WHEN YOU FEEL LIKE SCREAMING

Help for Frustrated Mothers

WHEN YOU FEEL LIKE
SCREAMING!
Help For Frustrated Mothers.

Pat Holt &
Grace Ketterman M.D.

Harold Shaw Publishers
Wheaton, Illinois

Cover art © 1988 by Gregory Eaton Clark

ISBN 0-87788-940-6

Library of Congress Cataloging-in-Publication Data

Holt, Pat, 1940–
    When you feel like screaming: help for frustrated
mothers/Pat Holt & Grace Ketterman.
       p. cm.
    Bibliography: p.
    ISBN 0-87788-940-6
    1. Discipline of children. 2. Child rearing.
I. Ketterman, Grace H. II. Title.
HQ770.4.H65 1988
649'.1—dc19   88-4978
                                   CIP

---

97 96 95 94 93 92 91 90 89

10 9 8 7

With love and gratitude
to the one who inspired this book,
and to all the precious children and mothers
who shared their thoughts and feelings
with such honesty and candor

Contents

Preface   ix

Acknowledgments   xi

Introduction   xv

1 When You Lose Control   1

2 For Reasonable Reasons   11

3 But It's Affecting Your Children   21

4 After the Storm   31

5 Mission Impossible?   37

6 How to Get Control of Yourself   45

7 Corralling Your Kids   57

8 The Key to Healing   69

Appendix   81

   Mothers' Questionnaire
   Survey Results

Preface

As you read this book, you may feel somewhat remorseful—even guilty—for the way you act around your kids. It is *not* our purpose to heap such painful emotions on you, but we do hope to help you recognize the damage screaming can do to your children, and to yourself.

As you become aware of the dangers, we challenge you to stop screaming at your kids and avoid the grieving aftermath. You *can* learn to get the attention of your children and to discipline them with gentle, firm control. Such control will help you to achieve the desired results without the emotional pain and scars that can damage both you and your children.

We do *not* promote permissiveness in childrearing. Nor do we advocate the saccharine sweetness and whiny patience that are neither honest nor effective. Your children will hear and heed you best when you speak clearly and firmly with short statements that are verified by the expression on your face and the tone of your voice. They combine to say to the child, "I say what I mean, and I mean what I say."

Perhaps you have never considered the intensity resulting from anger and the fear created by uncontrolled screaming as a form of child abuse. But it is. It may be conscious or unconscious, but it affects your family relationships. We'd like to offer you hope and some practical suggestions. We believe you can and would like to do better. That's why we wrote this book.

Pat Holt and Grace Ketterman, M.D.

Acknowledgments

This book was written with the help and encouragement of so many people. We are grateful to our editor, Ramona Cramer Tucker, for her enduring patience and consistent support. Joyce Farrell, our agent, believed in the project from the very start, and her enthusiasm never wavered.

A special word of thanks to Margie Friedenthal, whom we lovingly refer to as "Number One Critic." Her insightful comments challenged our thinking, and changed our direction.

Our deepest appreciation to our "Project Allies"—Nancy Barshaw, Linda Coyle, Cindy Hindman, Marilyn Silva, Yvonne Treydte, and Robyn Vander Weide.

A final benediction of thanksgiving to Liz George, who prayed this book to completion.

Screaming!

No Mom wants to,

but every mother feels like it.

SCREAMING!

If they'd be good . . .

If only they'd obey.

SCREAMING!

If only they would listen . . .

If only . . . If only . . .

Introduction

Dear Mother,

In preparation for a Mothers' seminar some time ago, we asked 150 nine-to-twelve-year-olds to answer anonymously two questions:

- What do you like most about your mother?
- What do you dislike most about your mother?

The answers were written without any further discussion.

Although the answers to the first question varied, the answers to the second did not. We were amazed. Almost every child used the phrase, "her screaming." Over and over again we read, "I can't stand it when she screams."

Recently we went into six 4th-, 5th-, and 6th-grade classrooms and told the children we needed their help in writing a book for mothers. We wrote the phrase, "Mommy, Please Stop Screaming!" on the chalkboard, and knowing giggles and sighs of understanding followed. Two hundred children knew exactly what "Mommy, Please Stop Screaming!" was about. Some of their stories are shared in this book so that we mothers can fully understand how our children see us and how our screaming affects them.

Mothers already know children "can't stand" screaming, and yet we continue to scream. Why? When? What are the factors that drive mothers to lose control?

We conducted a nationwide survey to answer these questions. The results of the survey and the responses of the mothers we interviewed are included in this book. The answers of these mothers demonstrate that regardless of the ages of the children, or the marital, professional, and socioeconomic status of the mothers, the reasons for screaming are the same.

Screaming is a habit, a habit that can be broken. Although the "screaming habit" breeds guilt in the mother, it can be difficult to break because many mothers are comfortable with the screaming (which usually guaranteees a certain measure of success) and tolerate the guilt that follows.

Why is it so hard to develop new behavior patterns? Changing behavior always involves risk. In the case of screaming, mothers risk leaving the comfort of the familiar habit with its predictable results for the unknown benefits of quiet control. This risk creates fearful anxiety, and anxiety makes the change difficult to attempt.

However, alternatives to screaming give such a high rate of success to the mother that her confidence level rises with continued use. Each successful experience will help the mother chip away at the wall of fear that keeps her from the personal confidence that ensures quiet control of herself and her children. Strong, controlled, confident women are capable and understanding mothers who raise confident and controlled children. We believe true strength is expressed only through gentleness and self-control. We look forward to journeying together with you in this book—to make you the best mother you can be.

Yours for keeping joy in motherhood,

Pat Holt and Grace Ketterman, M.D.

1

When You Lose Control

I met Kathleen* in the hallway. She was an attractive and intelligent woman in her early 40's and a business executive for a large corporation. She whisked me into her office and promptly shut the door. Then she began to tell me her story, with tears brimming in her eyes.

"I've alienated my children with my screaming," she cried. "My eighteen-year-old left home, my sixteen-year-old is there as little as possible, and when he is all we do is scream at each other. My four-teen-year-old withdraws. I can't communicate with her at all. And the younger ones—well, I'm losing them too." Her voice trailed off.

I discovered this woman has a history of severe hormonal imbalances which caused excessive mood swings. She is now under treatment which has considerably tempered her behavior. Yet she still screams; it's a habit. She's done it for years. Why? Are the children really so terrible?

"It's my husband," she sobbed. "I get so frustrated with him. After twenty years of disappointment, I can't stand it anymore. Then I lash out at my children, especially if I see them display any of his irresponsibility."

How do the children react? They turn away from her, even when

---

*names have been changed to maintain privacy

she tries to explain and defend herself. "They see my husband as the long-suffering hero," she complained.

Let's take a look at the facts in this situation. What are they? First, the mother screams. Why does she scream? For three reasons: because of her frustration with her husband that has compounded through the years; because she worries that her children may become "irresponsible" like her husband; and because she believes she screams because of her physical condition.

How does this screaming affect her relationships with her family? She told me that the children she loves have turned away from her. Her screaming also causes her children to overlook the father's faults and possibly to emulate them.

And what are the results of screaming in her life? She feels alienated and guilty. As her frustration grows more intense, what happens? She continues to scream.

What this lady described is a vicious cycle. She screams out of frustration, feels guilty because she has screamed, then does not know what to do about the guilt, and thus feels even worse. The worse she feels, the more she screams, and so the cycle gains control over her. It starts to destroy her and her relationships. Unless the harmful "screaming" pattern is broken, the damage resulting from the uncontrolled rage will scar future generations.

This is exactly what happened in Kent's* troubled family. Kent's mother screamed all the time. Not more than a day or two went by without his mother yelling at her five children. Kent lived in dread of her intense anger at even the slightest misdeeds. In fact, she even had screaming fits for which he could find no reason at all.

His mother also abused him physically. On one occasion, when he retorted rudely to his mother's yelling, she yelled even more. Then she told him she would whip him. Having had contact with her leather whipping strap before, Kent knew he wanted none of that, so he fled to the home of a new neighbor. He convinced them to let him spend the night. Time only fed the flames of his mother's fury. When he returned the next day, she greeted him with the strap and a stick.

Kent has never forgotten the pain of his punishments, the

1 egg
oatmeal

Sometimes
  its better
  to trade a
  soup of forgetful
          ness
  to cross the
  river to be
reborn on the
        other side

humiliation, helplessness, the fear and rage. They remain as emotional scars. He has tried to understand his mother, to forgive her, and to rise above the hurts her screaming inflicted, and so have the other children. But all of them have difficulty in their personal lives. There have been numerous divorces, and their children have suffered the fallout from their grandmother's rage.

Certainly Kent's mother was acting out the injustices of her own childhood. She screamed out of personal bitterness about needs that had never been met. She tried in unsuccessful ways to meet those needs, and then took out her pain and frustration on her helpless children.

No mother decides to be a screamer when she is tenderly holding her first precious newborn in her arms. So when do mothers scream? When does life become so frustrating that mothers lash out at their children in this way?

Through our study and experience we can pinpoint seven major reasons. Let's look at these together.

When Stress Becomes Too Great

Mothers scream when stress becomes too great. Listen to Mary's* story:

> My first mistake was choosing the day after school let out to start painting my kitchen. Next, I agreed to babysit a friend's six-year-old for the same week. My husband had been working overtime for about a year, so most of the family responsibilities fell on me. In the middle of this, we got a call from my husband's eighty-one-year-old grandmother saying she would like to come spend the summer with us. It seemed like a good idea at the time. I was also getting the last plans worked out for Vacation Bible School for which I was the Superintendent. I think if that was all that happened, I would have been fine, but that's not life.
>
> We received another phone call. A favorite uncle of mine was dying. I tried to "handle" everything myself. The next day I stood in the living room and screamed at my children—wanting to hit

them. Now I don't even remember what they did.

Had this mother been able to say, "No!" to the excessive demands and needs of others, she would probably not have reached the screaming breaking point. Children are a mother's dearest and most important responsibility, next to her husband. You must be careful to reserve your best for them and give to others whatever time and energy is left.

Let's face it. This may be easy to say, but it is extremely difficult to put into practice. But attempting to "do it all"—cramming too much into a day, a week, or a season—will result in stress overload. A mother must learn to say, "No!" to the needs of others when the needs of her family will be endangered by her saying, "Yes."

When There Are Too Many Demands on Limited Time

Mothers scream when they have too much to do in a limited time. Trish,* another busy mom, talks about the times she is most likely to scream:

> When I am late for an appointment or for work and there have already been endless interruptions from the telephone, my husband, and from the children. Then, as I am struggling to get the children to school on time, one of them tells me he forgot his lunch, homework, or whatever, and the other tells me she needs such and such for school today. Then I EXPLODE!

Preventing this sort of an explosion demands that a mother plan ahead. Getting up a little earlier, doing some food preparation the night before, and delegating duties to family members can work wonders in avoiding the frantic morning rush, as well as other stressful time periods.

Remember also, that through countless other times of pressure, you have made it. Knowing you will succeed again can help keep you calm and prevent screaming.

Too often an unwelcome, unnecessary incoming phone call

slows mothers down and ruins a perfectly good morning, after-noon, or evening schedule. Mothers can learn to avoid the "Tyran-ny of the Telephone." Some mothers refuse to be subject to the Tyrant Telephone and just don't answer the phone during peak crisis periods of the day. Their attitude is, "If it's important, they will call back!"

Mothers who are exceedingly curious or who must know who is calling for personal or business reasons should consider the invest-ment in an answering service or answering machine. It will save nerve strain and help to gain control of their time.

Other mothers train their children, as soon as they are account-able, to answer the phone and take a message. For younger children, this may be verbal. Older children can be responsible to take written messages. This book might never have been completed if Pat's children did not answer the phone, and say, "She is not avail-able right now. May I take a message?" They learned to say this at an early age and have been doing it consistently ever since. This particular wording works well—whether the mother is at home or away.

When She Doesn't Feel Well

Mothers scream when they do not feel well physically. Janet* remembers a time when she screamed because she didn't feel good:

> It was a difficult pre-menstrual time for me. My fourteen-year-old had been home sick the week before finals and had not opened a book. Since she is not a good student, she needs to study hard to make average grades. I had gone to a lot of trouble to get her books and assignments for her. She had a lot to do! Well, Saturday, she felt much better, put on her swim suit, and was going to sit in the sun to get a tan. She had NO plans to open a book! I exploded!

While pre-menstrual tension is well known to most women, few know that they can do something about it. Believe you can control yourself even during those difficult days. Watch your calendar! When those dark days draw nigh, monitor your diet carefully, avoiding salt that can make your body retain more fluids. This will help take away the "beached blimp" feeling that makes you even more tense and irritable. For some people, indulgences in sweets, especially chocolate, also aggravate unpleasant symptoms.

Mothers have a lot of demands on their time, and it's easy for them to get run-down, physically. It's also difficult because children bring colds and other illnesses home from school, and guess what? Mom is exposed to them all. Headaches, backaches, colds, "flu," and all sorts of aches and pains assail us.

When you feel ill or suffer from the tensions of PMS, listen to your body—it is warning you! Plan a lighter schedule if at all possible. Get extra rest. Simplify your life and say, "No!" when your emotional health is on the line. Avoid weighty decisions. Postpone decision-making until you feel better whenever possible. You'll be glad you did. Take more time than usual to handle personal and family situations. Do *not* give an ultimatum based on a hormonal imbalance!

There are many physical problems that can make your discomfort level high and your patience short. Take good care of yourself—you deserve it. This is good preventive medicine for busy moms. If and when you are ill, learn to simplify your life, organize your family to help, and practice special self-control so you will not feel worse from remorse than from your illness.

Sounds easy, you say. But you know it's hard in real life. You struggle with it. Just how do we go about simplifying and organizing? Don't despair. We'll look at some practical solutions in the next chapters.

When She Feels Helpless

Mothers scream when they feel helpless. Evelyn,* a 26-year-old single mother, expresses her frustration:

I am a single parent. My worst day came three weeks ago. My

employer told me I would not be needed as of the first of the month. My son's teacher told me that he continually disrupts the classroom, is aggressive on the playground, and just tried to forge my signature on a failing paper. Driving home in the rain, I got a flat tire, and no one stopped to help. About this time, my son asked if he could have a candy bar. That did it. I screamed longer and harder than I ever have in my life!

The proverbial straw that broke the back of the unsuspecting camel is a truth for mothers to consider. To avoid the relentless buildup of the weight of our pressures we must establish equilibrium. How can you do this? As one stress hits, deal with it instantly. Dealing with it means accepting the stress—*not* denying its existence. Find out what you can do about the stress, decide who can help you with it, and set a specific time when you will put the plan into motion. Then put that stress out of your mind. This will not eliminate the things that cause stress, but such planning will help you deal with them as they come along instead of letting them build up. It will also make you aware of your real strength and how to make that strength work for you.

When Her Children Don't Seem to Measure Up

Mothers scream when their children don't seem to be measuring up to their wishes or expectations. Terri,* a vivacious 30-year-old, told me this story:

A particular instance is written in my mind as if it were yesterday. On my doorstep appeared an outraged neighbor with her three-year-old boy who had a very red, long, ugly mark on his back. The mother raked me over the coals because my five-year-old son had hit her son. She was so angry. I was stunned by her outburst, and had nothing to say.

When I finally closed the door, I went after my son. He knew he was never to hit children, and so, without giving him a chance, I let him have it, screaming incessantly to vent my anger and disappointment. I was so mad. I never asked to hear his side of the story.

That story reminds Grace of the years she lived under the ugly cloud of others' expectations, feelings, and opinions of her and her children. It was a great day when she learned that her children were her first consideration. She found out how to explore with them what had really happened. Often they were not the only ones at fault. She learned to discipline more wisely and *much* more effectively when she discovered the value of listening instead of reacting without thinking.

When Her Children Remind Her of Someone Who Hurt Her

Mothers scream when their children consciously or unconsciously remind them of a difficult someone in their lives, someone who has hurt them. Jan* admitted,

> You'd better believe I scream when my ten-year-old-son shows any of the characteristics of the man who sired him, lied to me, and abandoned both of us in the hospital. I never want to see a trace of that man in my son!

This mother's words graphically illustrate the crucial need to work through every troubled relationship. Forgiveness and healing is an absolute necessity. Few families have no bothersome people in them. When a child has the misfortune to resemble that problem-person, it is very easy to displace bad feelings toward another person onto that child. Not only does the child suffer the consequences of his own misdeeds; he also suffers the results of old bitterness toward someone else. We will deal with the essential role of forgiveness in possessing a healthy emotional life and, specifically, in controlling screaming, in chapter seven.

From our study, we know not only when mothers are *most* likely to scream, but when they are *least* likely to scream.

One extremely frustrated mother said that she is least likely to scream when "everyone is asleep." Another told us, "I am least likely to scream when I have laryngitis!" Those familiar truths bring a chuckle to all of us.

The majority of mothers that we interviewed, however, are least likely to scream when:

- they are rested.
- things are calm.
- the children cooperate without complaint.
- they are "getting things done."
- there are other people around.

Because life is seldom ideal, mothers do scream. But there is hope. We have discovered that why mothers scream, what they verbalize, and the type of fundamental love and acceptance they express toward their children makes all the difference.

When She Fears Her Children May Go Wrong

Mothers scream when they fear their children may not grow up to be what or who they "should" be.

One mother screamed regularly at her seven children. Her daughter Nancy* recalls, "I dreaded her screamed-out lectures more than a spanking! Even now I can hear her shrill voice, disapproving manner, and the endless flow of words. I tried extremely hard to gain her approval, but I rarely felt I merited it."

There is a fascinating contrast between this mother and Kent's. Kent's mother seemed to take her rage at her own lot in life out on the children. This mother wanted her children to grow up into healthy, happy, and responsible adults and screaming was the only way she knew to help them to reach that place. But they could not understand that. Most of the time, she yelled because she desperately wanted her children to please God. She feared they might not measure up to His laws and could conceivably miss heaven in the end. Oh, if this mother had only realized the deep, deep love of Jesus and the provision he made for sin!

Somehow her love was transmitted to her children in spite of her screaming because they did try to please her. They became high achievers and conscientious adults, and all of them have unusual compassion for others.

In spite of the pain and trouble screaming causes, you may get by without serious results when you clearly love your children. Nevertheless, we believe you and your children will *feel* better and *do* better when you master different disciplinary skills. And that's what we'd like to share with you in the coming chapters of this book.

2

For Reasonable Reasons

I want to be heard so very badly because I care for my children. I love them so much, and want the best for them. If it takes volume to get the message across, that's what I use. I do what I have to do to get the message across.

These words are echoed by mothers all over the nation. It is ironic that the very results mothers yearn for fall short because they make a costly mistake—the mistake of screaming. The problem is that screaming *seems* to work. It certainly gets the children's attention, though it takes ever increasing volume to do it.

However, the lasting effect of screaming is that psychological callouses form on the eardrums. Louder and louder volume is demanded to obtain the desired result. After awhile, even screaming doesn't penetrate the wall that screaming has set up in the relationship between parent and child.

Of the many reasons mothers give for *why* they scream, nine stand out. We'll take them one at a time.

It Gets Their Attention

Why do many mothers scream? Just to get their children's attention.
Mandy* often feels exasperated with her son:

> When I speak to my thirteen-year-old son in a normal tone of
> voice, he doesn't even hear. It doesn't matter what I am saying. I
> usually repeat my request five or six times, and then I scream,
> "I'm talking to you—get over here!"
>
> His general attitude is that of disgust. He feels that I'm intrud-
> ing into his reverie, or TV program, etc. He is rarely doing his
> homework at times like this.
>
> Of course, when he finally grants me his attention, he
> answers, to whatever it is, "I can't now. I'm doing my
> homework."
>
> This makes me even more irritated, and I scream, "You've had
> four hours to do it!" etc.
>
> Then he sighs a big sigh and throws down his pencil. "Oh all
> right," he says grudgingly and slowly limps in my direction.

This boy is not likely to do whatever it is his mother asks. He
sounds angry, and his mother recognizes he is disgusted. Perhaps
that feeling is due to her intrusion, but we suspect it is aggravated
by the *way* she intrudes.

At thirteen, he is beginning to feel like a man and needs to be
treated more like one. Enduring Mom's yelling may remind him of
his early years. He may resent being treated like a child. How can
you treat an adolescent with respect for his time and interests and
yet get the job done? Here are a few tips.

The mother needs to talk with the boy as an individual rather
than as his commander. Respect for his schedule includes giving
him a broad base of time in which to accomplish the task she requests. That way, she demonstrates respect for whatever it is he is
doing, whether she approves of the expenditure of time or not. If he
has a voice in deciding when he will do assigned tasks, he is far more
likely to cooperate.

If at the end of the agreed-upon time the task is not completed, however, consequences must follow. Since both agreed on the work to be done, the consequences become the choice of the boy rather than an infliction from the mother. The consequences should be determined by what is important to the boy at his stage and also should be commensurate to his age.

Volume Will Drive the Message Home

Mothers hope that increased volume will get the point across more clearly, that it will make their children understand the message. Sarah,* a mother of five, felt that way:

> My ten-year-old daughter does not hear me unless I am in a higher decibel range. When I get her attention at long last, I speak clearly, firmly, and louder than usual. I always end with, "Do you understand me?" I do this to draw some kind of a response. Then I can always say later, "When we talked about this before, you said you understood."

Understanding a point is not enhanced by screaming. In fact, a child almost always perceives screaming as a synonym for anger. To children and adults as well, anger produces fear or anxiety. And fear commonly blocks learning. While the child may agree that she "understood," it may well be that she agreed in order to stop further screaming. So the important point the mother wants to make may be lost entirely. Exasperating, isn't it?

One nurse in a children's hospital has a very different means of getting a message home to a noisy, unheeding child. She draws the child close to her and whispers in his ear. Few children can resist wanting to hear a secret, and even the most troublesome child stops resisting, listens, and complies with her quiet request.

It Gets Results

Most mothers recognize that when they scream, their children get moving. Brenda* realized she used screaming to set fires under her slow-moving children.

My daughters needed to eat lunch quickly, and go to ballet. I told my nine-year-old to cover up her clothes in case she spilled. Of course she spilled her entire lunch over her leotard, then sauntered over to the sink to clean up. "Wipe it up thoroughly. We must get going!" Still slow action. I turned up the volume— "GET MOVING!"— and got results.

My eleven-year-old daughter was sitting barefoot at the table, half-consciously picking at her food without making any headway. Time was a consideration, so in order to get action I turned up the volume. "Move, kid!" That sent her flying out the door, socks in mouth, and a shoe in each hand. Not nastiness but the vocal push helped the go-cart go!

Screaming is not *always* bad. In an emergency it will produce action. The problem with yelling habitually, however, is that of the proverbial shepherd boy who loudly and habitually cried "Wolf!" to get the attention and comfort of other people. When a wolf really appeared no one believed him, and the wolf killed a sheep.

Screaming stimulates nervousness in children. We know that a parent's irritation can be a factor in spilling and breaking things. Children actually slow to a standstill because they dread the next level of Mom's anger. Understandably enough, moms see this as stubbornness or even defiance. Perhaps remembering how you felt as a child when someone yelled at you can help you understand your child better.

Logically, a child should get moving toward compliance to avoid repeated yelling. But the child's emotions interfere with logical thinking. If you want to stop screaming and yet gain your child's obedience and respect, put yourself in her shoes. If you felt like she does, what would work? How would you learn to give those desired results? Then try out your own new ideas! You may discover some wonderful techniques that really work for you and your child.

To Show Them How Their Behavior Affects Me

Many mothers are just trying to help their children understand how much their behavior affects them. Gini* felt that way.

> My daughter was two-and-a-half-years-old, in the middle of potty training. I was eight months pregnant and feeling very tired and immobile. I was worn out from trying to meet my daughter's physical needs. I had used all the encouraging words. Finally I couldn't physically keep up with her demands. "Go to the bathroom now, honey. You can do it." She wouldn't go. She stood there in front of me, arms folded, and wet her pants through everything. I knew it was defiance. I became furious and made her sit in her own puddle until I could cool down. I did more than a reasonable amount of screaming!

One of the negative results of regular screaming is the creation of walls of resentments between mother and child. The resentment is mixed with anxiety, and young children have no words for expressing these profound, often intense, feelings. They are left to act them out in one of two ways: They become aggressive, or "hyper," and begin yelling themselves, or they withdraw in silent resistance. Often they role-play their responses while playing with other children.

At no age, perhaps, is this more evident than in the two's. The mother of a two-year-old who struggles with the screaming habit would be wise to postpone potty training for a while. Even though there would be extra work involved, both the mother and her child would be far better off in the long run. The toilet-training process might have been much less stressful for Gini and her daughter if Gini had waited until after she had the baby and was more comfortable physically. They could probably have avoided the emotional barrier-building of Mom's anger. That little girl would learn to use the potty in due time.

It is important for children to understand how parents feel, but it is even more important that the children do not feel guilty for causing a parent's bad feelings. Gini blamed her daughter's seemingly deliberate wetting as a personal attack on her. The physical discomfort and the pressure to toilet train her child before the arrival of a new baby pushed her to her breaking point. The combination of factors—not the two-year-old—unleashed her angry screaming.

Although she screamed, Gini wisely chose to take time to "cool down" before she took action. That cooling-down time can be a lifesaver. Discipline yourself to think about all the facts and feelings in any tense situation. Avoiding blame will help you handle life more effectively.

I Feel Better

When mothers scream, it releases the building anger and frustration—for the moment. Mary Lou,* a homemaker and part-time secretary, shared this with me:

> Maybe I am unique in this area, but I am deeply affected by behaviors such as irresponsibility and undependability. They go against my nature. When I see my children displaying such behavior, or leaning in this direction, I try to say to myself, "They're not like me. I need to accept them as they are." But it doesn't work. Sooner or later I scream, and it does make me feel better because I'm so frustrated. I'm venting my frustration in the sense that when I scream at my children about irresponsibility, I am yelling at my husband, "You are allowing this thing to happen. You are allowing mediocrity, and I cannot accept this. I don't want the children to turn out like you."

Some mothers feel much better after screaming. But sooner or later, they yell again—proof that the good feeling does not last. So don't let that temporary good feeling deceive you! We hope to help you find lasting joy and peace of mind in your parenting skills.

It is especially devastating to children to feel that one parent criticizes or puts down the other. When the child's misbehavior is likened to the "bad" parent's, that child experiences an upheaval of emotions. The child is hurt by and angry with the yelling parent. The child fears he is no good and that the other parent is no good either. The child believes he is doomed to become an adult who is "bad like dad," so he feels hopeless and helpless. Anger, sadness, guilt, fear, and helplessness are the well-defined ingredients of depression. This price tag for a mother to feel temporarily better after screaming is simply too high.

There are successful ways to help your children become fine adults. Your disappointments and frustrations regarding their dad will have to be worked out. Please refer to chapter eight on forgiving. There is great hope for you!

It's Better Than Hitting Them

These mothers are correct—screaming *is* better than hitting their children. This was something that Angie,* a shy 40-year-old homemaker, struggled with.

I've been responsible for my stepdaughter since she was four years old. To the best of my ability, I have always been available to give her motherly love and advice. Her father adores her. On one particular occasion during her teen years, we had taken her on a trip. She was glad to take everything we offered, but when her dad wanted her to go somewhere with him, she wasn't interested because she wanted to spend time with a boy.

I tried to support her father by insisting, pointing out that we had indulged her every whim and that she should do something for her father. I felt strong rejection from her, and she screamed, "I don't have to listen to you! You're not my mother!"

I couldn't take any more and so I screamed back, "I'm glad I'm not your mother!" Believe me, I felt like hitting her!

Getting out one's frustrations by screaming rather than hitting is commendable! Child abuse is a tragedy—it impacts the lives of so many families in a destructive way. But we have good news for you. You do not need to resort to either hitting *or* yelling. There are other choices.

In this situation, both stepmother and father need to work together. The facts seem to indicate that dad, who "adores her," may unwittingly have pampered his daughter. Most mothers rightfully resent such spoiling, but out of love and respect for their husbands (or helplessness to open his eyes!) they keep quiet and take their resentment out on the child.

Rather than yelling or hitting, this mother and dad could have asked for a few minutes alone. A calm, clear statement from Mother reflecting this girl's ingratitude and selfish, demanding ways might have opened Dad's eyes. Out of concern for this girl's future relationships and character, they could have come up with a plan to help her. Grounding her for the evening from all fun could have taught her a much needed lesson. Mom and Dad could have had a nice time, and almost certainly this daughter would behave better next time.

I Learned It from My Mother

Many mothers, either consciously or unconsciously, struggle in a cycle of abuse learned during their childhoods. Can you identify with Tina*?

> My mother was a screamer, and looking back it seems to me that all she ever did was yell at my sister and me. Now both of us have children of our own. One thing we never wanted to do was be like her, and yet it has happened. Our children call us, "The Screaming Duet." We feel like such utter failures. I can't believe we've turned out to be just like that woman.

In chapter one, we described Kent's mother and her screaming pattern. His sister revealed that, to her horror, she too yelled at her children. Every time she did, she ended up in tears of remorse and with painful memories of her childhood. She worked heroically to break that habit and was able to find more successful means to train her children.

Most people parent in one of two ways—either like their own

parents or in a totally opposite style. If you had a mother who yelled, it may be much harder for you to stop than if you had not grown up with screaming.

Screaming Seems Powerful

Many mothers told us that screaming made them feel powerful.

Susan* and I sat across from each other in McDonalds. As we ate our burgers, we chatted about our children and the frustrations we felt. She hung her head and focused intently on her fries as she said:

> Most of the time my childrearing efforts seem futile. Usually I accept being taken for granted and am rather passive. But on certain occasions, with enough provocation, I get very angry and really let the children have it. Perhaps I shouldn't admit this, but I get a sense of power that comes with my anger and my screaming at those times.

Raising children properly in today's stressful times is not easy. When too many burdens pile up on you, you may fear that you just can't cope. You are likely to feel inept, weak, or inadequate. It is extremely likely that you will discover a sense of power when you yell. That feeling seems much more desirable than those negative emotions. Before you realize it, you can develop the screaming habit.

Remember our philosophy: True strength is always gentle—and real gentleness is strong.

I Feel Desperate

Some mothers scream because they reach a desperation point. Carrie,* who got married at eighteen, talked about her marriage and family.

> Nothing has turned out the way I planned. I had the same

hopes and dreams every little girl has of being pursued by Prince Charming, getting married, and living happily ever after. Instead I settled for a weakling, supported him through school, had the children, took care of him and the children, and then was left when he got tired of "all the responsibility." Yes, I scream. I scream at shattered hopes and broken dreams.

Any mother can feel desperate at times, but those who are especially vulnerable to that extreme condition are single moms. They heroically struggle to maintain a home by working long hours and then face all of the demands of child rearing alone. We know few who have resolved the hurts and anger left from a divorce, and many of the mannerisms of their children remind them of their ex-husband.

The personal losses of a marriage, financial support, and social position, plus the immense responsibilities that must now be shouldered alone combine to create near-impossible living. It is necessary to find some support if you are to avoid taking out your frustration on your children.

If you will look around, you will find many moms who suffer from nearly identical problems. They need support, too. We suggest you find other single mothers and plan creatively some means of alternating child care now and then to permit some personal time for each mother. Assisting each other with budgeting, hearing solutions others have discovered, and *occasionally* allowing time simply to communicate can take the edge off your stress. You will find it far more possible to be firm, consistent, and reasonable with your children if you enjoy this sort of support system.

You may have a reason for yelling that we haven't discovered. Whatever the reason, we believe it's not good enough to excuse your continuing to scream. As you read on, you will learn how children react to mothers' screaming and why you need to find another method to get them to do what you want them to do.

3

But It's Affecting Your Children

There is a wide disparity between how parents *believe* their children react to their screaming and how the children actually respond. Mothers do not want their children to think of their yelling or screaming in a negative way.

I was devastated to discover that my children thought that I screamed a lot. Perhaps it is just that they take my screaming more seriously than I intend. I wish that they could understand screaming is not just a way of getting my point across but is also my way of ventilating pent-up frustration.

This parent feels her yelling serves two purposes: It gets her point across and it ventilates her "pent-up frustration." It would be nice if children could understand adults better. When mothers take time to explain their moods and yelling to children, it helps, but children who are hurt, afraid, or anxious cannot get beyond themselves to comprehend the entire situation. It is unrealistic to expect them to understand emotions that adults themselves have difficulty handling.

We urge you moms who are habitual screamers to try to explain your feelings to your children. When you are not upset and can remain calm, take time to talk together. Tell them you are anxious to teach them responsibility, good behavior, and excellence in how they do their work. Help them understand that at times you get worried that you aren't doing as good a job as you'd like and then you find yourself screaming to *make* them respond. You may, of course, have a different explanation, but interpreting your actions will help your children respect you and enable them to be less hurt when you do scream.

Unfortunately, the emotional distress that children experience is not the only result of a mother's screaming. Like it or not, children learn from example and will emulate what they hear and observe. A screaming mother signals to the young child that screaming is an acceptable form of communication, and all too soon the child begins to respond by screaming back. This screaming chain is self-perpetuating, and it becomes a highly developed and unfortunate habit deeply ingrained in the personality of the child.

Children respond to screaming in one or more of the following ways.

Sadness and Hurt Feelings

This fifth-grade student poignantly describes her sad and hurt response to her mother's yelling:

> *That really breaks my heart when she yells or screams like that. I'd just wish she was just not a yeller or screamer. I wish that she would be a little more tender and nice.*

This child makes it very clear that mom's screaming "breaks my heart." It is almost certain that *every* child feels pain at first when a mother screams. Through a variety of protective devices, they learn to stop hurting and adapt to the inevitable yelling over which they have no control.

Pain in any child will cause one of three responses: (a) the child will withdraw and suffer the pain in silence; (b) he or she will learn to cover the pain with a facade of indifference or anger; or, (c) he or she is likely to escape from the mother emotionally and even physically. We will discuss these reactions in more detail in this chapter.

Angry Back-talk

A fourth-grade boy wrote this personal experience:

Once my brother was playing the piano and he hit a wrong note and my mommy hit his hand. My brother said mom why did you do that? My mommy said because you hit a wrong note. So my mom screamed at my brother and my brother screamed at my mommy. They went on screaming until my daddy got home. I think my brother felt mad. My mommy could of handeled it better by saying Alex, try another note or by saying Alex, you touched one wrong note.

The child who wrote this story is requesting that his mother exert more patience and self-control—an appropriate and logical request. But self-control in the heat of frustration is very difficult.

This mom screamed because her son's piano playing did not meet her expectations, and her son reacted by yelling back. Obviously he felt angry and resented her screaming. Sadly, the mother defeated her well-intentioned objective (helping her son learn and achieve) by the method she used (screaming). In fact if this boy had really wanted to become a pianist, he may well have rebelled and failed to reach that goal because of the anger created by such screaming matches.

The ill will created by mothers' screaming extends into the adult life as the following story illustrates. Only recently, Helen,* an adult daughter of a mother who screamed at her, returned to her home town to visit her brothers. She decided that she would not visit her mother or even call her. Believing their mother would be hurt if her daughter failed to reach out to her, the brothers prevailed on her to phone their mom.

Helen had learned to scream at her own children and husband, and she hated this trait in herself as much as she had in her mother. So when she called her mother, the two of them promptly engaged in an angry yelling match on the telephone. The mother accused, "I guess I just don't have a daughter any more!" Pathetically, Helen screamed back, "Mom, there were plenty of times I felt I didn't have a mother!"

Helen illustrates several reactions to her mother's screaming— yelling back, drawing out fear and dread of the habitual anger, and leaving home early (she went to live with relatives as a young teenager).

Screaming, in the long run, has a painful, negative payoff.

Fear and Withdrawal

Some children are sensitive and easily intimidated by others' intensity. One such child's attempt to help his mother backfired.

One night I tried to do the wash as a favor. But I didn't know what I was doing. My mom was upset and started to scream. Her best skirt was ruined. I think if she would of had more temperance she wouldn't of screamed. I felt like running away. I hid behind the dresser. But I came out because I was hungry.

This child states clearly that running away was a strong temptation. An adult friend, a victim of a yelling mother told us that he, his sister, and his brother left home in their mid-teens. They did so because they could no longer tolerate what they experienced as abuse—their mother's screaming.

If you are a screaming mom and it seems to be working, reconsider! While your children may tolerate your yelling and even comply with your requests when you yell, they may be storing away the pain and resentment until they can escape it all. Look into the years ahead. If your child continues to react as he or she is now, what could happen to her ten years from now? Keeping that question in mind has often helped us to avoid screaming at our own children.

Angry, Sullen Silence

The silence of anger is very different from that of sadness and hurt. Many children quickly identify an almost unbeatable weapon against a screaming mother: they ignore her in quiet, seething anger.

I went to school once. I had a sandwich with manaise and I hate manaise and she knows it so I didn't eat it. When I got home my mom screamed at me. I went to my room and ignored her for the rest of the day.

When a child yells back a verbal fight ensues in which neither child nor parent really wins. In such a fight, however, both express feelings and there is a certain equality of power—however negative it is.

But when a child withdraws into angry silence, the balance in the power struggle tips in the child's favor. The results are often tragic. Such silent anger sometimes increases a mother's anger and leads to abuse. A mother, desperate to win the combat, may resort to physical violence to "break the will" of her child. But she usually breaks her child's heart and the bonds that tie her child to her instead.

Every time I'm watching my favorite T.V. show my mommie tells me to do chores. I asked her if I could do them later. She has to scream, "Get in here young man and do your chores!" I hate it when my mommie screams. It makes me feel as if I am two inches tall. Just because she screamed she is in a bad mood and when I get screamed at I'm in a bad mood. Mommie please, stop screaming.

This child's story reveals a common combat zone between parents and children—that of giving up pleasure and substituting work. Mothers are correct in trying to teach their children to be responsible. But screaming is not an appropriate teaching technique! Children are likely to feel "two inches tall"—quite helpless and worthless. Good parenting demands building into children the qualities of worth, confidence, and respect. Prolonged efforts at instilling these traits into children can be undone by a few episodes of screaming which, for the moment at least, made this child feel worthless.

Humiliation and Shame

Just as certain sensitive children react to mothers' screaming with fear, others respond with humiliation and shame. The most serious, deep, and painful humiliation and shame occur when a mother's yelling comes in the presence of a friend. Both the child and his friend were "uneasy" or embarrassed in the following example.

My friend's mom is constantly screaming at him for no reason, but sometimes he is bad like the time he through a pail of water over her head. When that happened, all she did was scream. I don't know about him, but it made me feel uneasy. I think she should be more calm. At least try. Then I think she should have punished him because all screaming does is make him nervous and not want to trust her anymore.

These humiliating experiences are more common than we like to think. Grace remembers one of her own.

I shall never forget one experience of shame from my own mother's yelling. When I was in the first grade, I was in the Christmas program at school. Dressed in our Sunday best, we were all lined up on the stage to sing Christmas carols for our parents and interested neighbors. Only one child among us wore new clothes since that Christmas occurred in the depths of the big Depression. This child stood beside me as we sang, and I became enchanted with the fuzzy yarn balls at the ends of the bow tied at the neck of her gorgeous golden sweater. Finally I could resist no longer. I reached over, not missing a note, and touched those delightfully soft miniature pom-poms.

The next morning during breakfast my mother lectured me resoundingly about my behavior. She told me that she had been embarrassed and that the entire audience had laughed. She went on at some length. When I could, I crept away and hid behind the kitchen stove. I doubt a criminal sentenced for a crime could feel worse than I did that day. Like the child in the other story, I did "not want to trust her any more."

Fortunately, there was a redemptive ending to that situation. My father left the table and searched until he found me. He lifted me up in his strong arms, looked at me with tender brown eyes and said, "Gracie, I didn't think it was so bad! In fact, it was kind of cute!" Never again did he ever counter one of mother's screams, but that one time was enough to restore hope and even self-respect.

Mothers, let us make this a plea! Don't yell at your children in a way that robs them of the self-esteem that is so essential to the emotional health you want them to develop.

Children Form a Coalition Against Mother

My children seem to "gang-up" on me. If I only had to deal with one at a time, I'm sure I could do okay. But when all three of them get together, how can I cope with them?

In this case, further investigation revealed a mom who sincerely wanted her children to become respectful, well-behaved people. Her methods of stretching for that goal, however, were responsible for their coalition of rebellion. She spoke loudly, threatened, and shamed the children, and did so openly in front of all of them. The victim looked to the others for sympathy and support and invariably received a wink or a gesture that met his needs. In turn, he gave similar sympathy to his sister and brother. As time went on, they became companions not only in punishment but also in new acts of mischief.

Mothers, please stop screaming. Find the time to take a child who needs correction to a place of privacy. Gain the self-control you need to explain what was wrong, how to correct it, and what you will do to help make the right things happen. We will discuss other corrective measures later.

Indifference or Laughter

When children endure screaming frequently, they often learn to act as if they don't care. I have heard children say, "Mom, I've heard that lecture so many times, I know it by heart!" It seems that children develop an attention block so they actually do not hear their mothers' yelling. Such indifference, real or feigned, can further infuriate moms who are already upset!

One friend, however, tells this truly remarkable story. Her mother was left alone a great deal because of her husband's work. Single-handedly she struggled to raise six children, and she yelled a *lot* in the process.

This friend's little brother seemed to get more than his share of their mother's yelling. One day, she really let him have it, and he stoically heard her out. He was only six, but when she finally became calm, this gentle child said, "Mommy, you really hurt my feelings when you yell, but I still love you!"

Whatever your child's reaction to your screaming may be, please consider stopping. The scars and callouses it creates in your child can be difficult to erase—if not impossible.

4

After the Storm

Episodes of screaming are always two-party encounters. We've discussed how *children* react to their mothers' screaming. Now we need to explore how *mothers* feel after screaming. When asked on the survey, most mothers replied with one of the four emotions we'll discuss in this chapter.

Guilt

Guilty is the self-imposed verdict of an overwhelming majority of mothers we questioned. When asked how they feel after a screaming session, again and again the mothers wrote, "Guilty."

As painful as guilt is, it serves a most useful purpose! In fact, because it is so painful, guilt is a powerful motivator for change. We were glad to discover that so many moms were honest enough to admit they feel guilty.

There are several reasons for this sense of guilt which will help you understand yourselves and each other better. Through understanding comes forgiveness and the capacity to change your habits.

I lost control

My four-year-old doesn't deserve to be screamed at. He's hurt and confused, and I'm left guilty.

I feel guilty and out of control. My twelve-year-old daughter will look at me as if to say, "Here she goes again," and plug her ears. She has also told me that I don't love her because I scream.

I feel guilty that I have vented my frustration, but with no positive results.

I feel guilty because it usually means I overreacted to the situation.

I feel guilty because I allowed circumstances to control me.

I feel terribly guilty. One Saturday I screamed so loud and long at my fourteen-year-old it ruined our entire weekend. We all cried and cried. It took me three days to feel good about myself again. That day I apologized to everyone, asked for their forgiveness, had a long talk with my daughter, prayed with her, etc. But only God can repair the damage I *did* to my relationship with her. I wounded her deeply. I feel like a total failure as a mom.

What else could I do?
I feel guilty. I often wonder why I keep making the same mistakes instead of learning from them and becoming more effective in quietly communicating with my children.

I feel so inadequate
I feel guilty and inadequate. I have usually said something I wish I hadn't—something that was an exaggeration of the problem. I fear that I have given the children (ages ten, six, and four) negative impressions of themselves. I have failed to be a good example, and have been inadequate in dealing with the problem.

I feel guilty and disappointed in myself—plus I usually don't get over my anger as fast as when I deal calmly with the children.

There is a major danger in permitting an ongoing sense of guilt to overwhelm you. Children *do* need correction and discipline, so don't believe for one minute we are advocates of permissive, passive child-rearing practices! We just want to help you avoid pitfalls that may defeat you.

Grace vowed, even as a child, that *she* would never yell at *her* children. But the time came when she broke that vow and yelled at her seven-year-old son. When she had finished, she sent him to his room to think it over.

He was not the one who did the most thinking, however. Grace suddenly saw in his remorseful young face her own childish feelings when her mother yelled. She began to consider his age and size and believed she had been unrealistic in her expectations. In fact, Grace became so remorseful and guilt-ridden that she took action.

She placed a slice of her son's favorite chocolate cake and a glass of cold milk on a tray. Bearing this offering of condolence and reparation, she went to his room where he was leaning over his desk in pensive thought. As that perceptive lad realized what his mom had done, he said, "Mom, you just spoiled the whole thing!" In this case, he was wiser than his mother and realized he needed the correction.

It was guilt and over-identification with her son that resulted in Grace's mistake. Screaming wasn't the answer, but rewarding the child with cake wasn't the answer, either. Life is a constant search for balances in too much, too little, too soon, and too late. Admittedly it isn't easy to find that midpoint, but most of us can be better than we are. In the last chapter we will offer you some help with your struggles over guilt.

Shame or Embarrassment

Guilt was the mothers' number one feeling after screaming. The next reaction of moms to their own screaming was shame or embarrassment.

As I grew up with a screaming mother, I hate it, and I hate myself for repeating such shameful behavior. I don't believe that instilling fear is a useful form of discipline—yet that's what screaming does.

I feel ashamed and more upset because I know my screaming only adds to the problem.

I feel very unhappy, and ashamed of myself. To make matters worse, my sixteen- and fifteen-year-olds check the calendar to see if it's close to my monthly grouch time!

If you are one of the mothers who feel such shame and remorse, count yourself fortunate. Like guilt, shame can prompt you to change. Since it is a painful emotion, we work very hard to overcome and avoid it.

When you feel embarrassed, you may very well begin to understand your children. They too feel embarrassed and shamed when you yell at them. So as you overcome your shame, perhaps you will be able to help your children heal from their embarrassment. Together you can grow in self-control, the genuine strength of true gentleness, and the self-respect we all need.

Obviously to avoid the shame, you will need to break your habit of screaming and replace it with new methods of training and discipline. In chapters six and seven, we'll give you some guidelines.

Release — I Feel Better

Several perceptive and honest mothers admitted to feeling "better" after yelling at their children. Screaming seemed to relieve their tension and frustration temporarily—later they experienced guilt or shame.

Usually it makes me feel better to "blow off steam." But after a little while I feel guilty, and I realize that there could have been a much better way to handle the situation. I end up having to apologize to my children for my wrong behavior.

Right after I scream I feel like justifying myself. Yes, I really did have a reason to get angry. It was the last straw. Then we go from there—we apologize, discuss, and then lay it to rest, permanently. I always hated it when my mom reminded me how bad I'd been two hours or two days or two weeks or two years ago. In my home, we aim to forget the problem and move on!

After releasing their emotions, these mothers feel calm. One child described his mom after a time of screaming as being "normal" for several days. He endured her yelling for the blessed respite from her anger, that period of calm after the storm.

While some moms are aware of the onslaught of remorse after they experience the relief, many are not so fortunate. A mother might enjoy the relief and remain unaware that she leaves her children devastated by helpless, sad, frightened, and angry feelings. She may only perceive her children as more compliant, or, because they withdraw, "out of her hair."

If you are one of these moms, please step back and take a look at yourself. We know that you *do* love your children. We suspect you simply have not recognized what your explosive lectures are doing to them. You can change. We hope you will try!

A Sense of Power

In chapter two we described why mothers scream. One of the reasons is the sense of powerlessness many mothers experience. When Anne* was asked how she felt after screaming, she replied that she discovered "a sense of power that comes with anger." Obviously it *is* anger that prompts yelling. Melissa* agreed with Anne:

After feeling so completely frustrated, screaming restores the sense of power to me, makes me feel that I really am in charge of the situation. Of course, this feeling passes rapidly, and I am back to feeling helpless.

It seems that the answer to this set of mothers' responses is the acquisition of true strength. Since they use angry screaming to work up a sense of power, it is apparent that they feel helpless and are trying desperately to bolster their areas of weakness.

It is encouraging to realize that everyone is given some assets. We only have to recognize them, choose to develop them, and use them. But it is fear and inexperience that defeat us, and usually these grow out of the helpless years of our childhood. Learn to recognize your needs and feelings. Name and discuss them until you catch them *before* you resort to the deceptive power of screaming to cover them.

For example, if you feel weak and uncertain, why not admit it? Your child no doubt senses that anyway and will respect you more, not less, for admitting your anxiety. Say something like this, "Sally, when you fail to stop watching TV to do your jobs and schoolwork, I feel worried and sad. Because I do so much for you, I'd like you to show me your appreciation by helping me. I worry about your future when you seem to care so little about learning and being responsible." Having spoken honestly about your own feelings, you might ask your Sally or Jim how they feel and if they'd like to see some changes. Try to involve them in solutions to *your* concerns about *their* problems that can eliminate your screaming.

Whether you feel guilty, ashamed, powerful, "better," or a mix of these emotions, you need to pay attention to your feelings. Understanding how screaming makes you feel is one of the keys to finding a way to stop.

5

Mission Impossible?

Please help me. I don't want to scream, really I don't. Each time it happens, I tell myself that I'll work harder to change, that it won't happen again, and yet it always does. Why do I keep doing what I hate?

According to our experience and investigation, all children and most mothers hate screaming. We have just discussed the many profoundly negative feelings that result from screaming episodes. Guilt, sadness, shame, anger, and a desire to hide or run away are only a few of the painful reactions to screaming. So why do mothers continue to yell? What makes it so difficult to stop?

Habit

When I think of my mother, I see her screaming at my brother or me over something trivial and always—always—making big issues out of inconsequentials. My mother felt the same way about my grandmother, and now my children tell me that I over-react and continually make a big deal over nothing!

When certain habits become ingrained in a person's lifestyle, they become extremely hard to break. When those habits have extended through generations of a family, the patterns become even more difficult to change.

But there is hope. Any habit can be broken. No matter what the underlying reason for those habits may be (and we will discuss those next), you can break them. Of course, first you must want to. But more importantly you must *decide* to. You will need a specific plan not only to stop your yelling but also to substitute a more successful, new habit. In chapter six, we will outline a simple plan for you to use.

Lack of Knowledge about Alternatives

Because of family habit patterns, most of us parent our children in one of two ways—*like* our parents or *opposite* from them. Either extreme may be equally erroneous. The mother who grows up with a screaming mother will often vow never to scream. However, she may overreact by becoming too passive and end up being thought of as a "wimp" by her children.

There are four sources for learning about new and different parenting skills. *Television*, if viewed thoughtfully, can teach both positive and negative modes of parenting. *Books* and *articles* can give excellent ideas on good discipline and training skills. *Other parents* (good or bad) can provide a rich source of different techniques in handling children. *Your own parental instincts* can guide you in many situations. Be careful, however, to differentiate the God-given quality of instinctive parenting from your own impulsiveness.

An example of personalized parenting came from a friend. Her teenage son had lied, and she could not get him to admit it or tell the truth, which she had accidentally discovered. At her wit's end, she quietly came into his room where he was sitting, sullen and stubborn on his bed. Matter-of-factly she said, "Tom, neither of us is going to leave this room until you tell me what you really did."

She sat quietly beside him with only an occasional comment for well over two hours. There was no nagging, screaming, or coercion, and at last Tom's defensiveness broke. The true story poured out with his genuine shame and remorse. Together they planned a means of correcting his misdeed, and later he followed through with the plan.

Children themselves offer some wise alternatives to screaming. While we may not agree to allowing children to place their responsibilities second to TV viewing, there is some wisdom in these suggestions from children. Listen to Laurie's* story:

My Mom usually screams at me when I am soposed to be cleaning the hamster cage but I am playing something or watching T.V. Then she says "GET OVER HERE!" and she starts screaming at me, and I start talking back to her and we get in a big fight, and she usually wins and I get grounded. I think that my mom could have let me clean the hamster cage when the T.V. program was over.

How often mothers scream because they are overwhelmed with fatigue and heavy responsibilities! Elizabeth,* a fourth grader, makes a suggestion that's right on target.

One Tuesday after school I was watching television. When my mom came home she was a real bad mood. She walked in the door and turned off the television. Then took the madness out on me by screaming at me. I felt realy bad for the rest of the day. I think my mom could have took a nap to get around screaming. There is always a way to get around screaming.

Lack of Self-Control

Interestingly, it is often in an attempt to teach self-control to children that mothers lose their own control. Recently I received a letter from a mother (much like the mother we discussed earlier) who was desperate about her two-year old's toilet training. She would sit with him while he was on his potty for a long time with no results—only to have him immediately make a mess in his clean diaper. Once she "lost it" and, to her horror, began screaming at him and shaking him. Many mothers lose control over problems that are even less distressing than dirty diapers during potty-training.

Self-control begins as the product of good, external controls exerted by parents on young children. The first three years are by far the most important era of life. During those first crucial months, children learn to control their physical functions—to sit, crawl, and walk. Then they learn to eat, and they finally gain bowel and bladder control.

At two, toddlers learn to say "no!" to almost every request of their mothers. Soon they learn to bend their wills and adapt to the demands of family living. The temper tantrums common to almost all toddlers have much to do with their need to test adult controls and pit their wills and wishes against their parents. It is extremely important for parents to exert healthy authority over a child if he or she is to learn self-control. The best control possible, by the way, is that of lovingly but very securely holding that child until the tantrum is over. It is exactly such loving, tangible, external control that first enables a young child to begin to exert self-control.

The next stage of self-control is acquiring a sense of responsibility. By kindergarten age, children must learn to take turns, share, and cooperate with others. They must assume major responsibilities for themselves, such as doing school work and performing a number of tasks about their homes. All of these jobs demand a great deal of self-control.

During adolescence control extends to social behaviors and is extremely important in handling sexual feelings and desires. The need to collaborate in team sports, school groups, and on part-time jobs requires great self-control.

Those who reach adult life without mastering the skill of self-control are likely to be in all sorts of difficulty. Certainly they are at risk to be screaming parents. To develop self-control as an adult on your own is a heroic task. Nevertheless, it *is* possible, and we urge you to work at it. Chapter six will give specific steps to help you master this skill.

Lack of Motivation

Several mothers told us they believed that screaming worked. Why? Because their children would finally obey them when they yelled. Others felt powerful, as if they had finally gained control over their children. So why should they change?

We can give a very good reason—the cost of screaming's apparent success is just too high. All mothers are familiar with determining whether a cost is reasonable. Maybe the dazzling new outfit you'd love to have simply won't fit your budget. The luxury of convenience foods is tempting, but you know the total bill would horrify you at the grocery check-out counter.

That's the way it is with screaming. It *seems* powerful and successful, but the price includes resentments, fears, and a silent vow for revenge in your child. As soon as he or she is bigger or feels more powerful than you, there will be a showdown—and no one will win.

So think carefully and with a long-range perspective. If you do, we believe you will become motivated to change your habits of screaming.

Failure to Understand the Power to Choose

As a psychiatrist, Grace has become impressed with the many people who do not realize they can *choose*—not only how they will act and react, but how they will feel as well. One patient told her that the most important fact he had learned in forty-five years of life is that very one: "I can choose!" The gift of choice was given to people by the Creator, but many not only fail to recognize it, they fail to use it and benefit from doing so.

We have so little control over many things that happen to us, but we do have ultimate control over how we will respond to those happenings. When a child breaks your favorite vase or tears a precious book while you are on the telephone, you can decide: Will you rage at the child in your frustration? Or will you calmly and firmly teach that parts of the house and special items demand different behaviors? "You do not throw a ball near the shelf where pretty things are arranged!" Or, "You do not treat books carelessly!" You may even need to exercise the choice of putting certain items out of reach of young children until they learn to be careful.

To master the art of choosing how you will feel instead of blindly reacting, try these steps:

1. Identify clearly whatever feeling you are experiencing.
2. Determine why you feel that way.
3. Decide what you will do to correct the problem and erase the emotion.
4. Follow through with the action.

There is always something we can do about any situation. Sometimes it is only our own attitudes and responses over which we have control. If so, then exercise that in the most positive, constructive way possible.

Choosing how you respond does not mean that you become so "patient" that you end up being permissive. It only means that you will react firmly, clearly, and fairly so your children will benefit from your healthy authority.

Ricky* said he felt "bad for the thing I did wrong, but she (mommy) doesn't have to scream. She can say, 'Please don't watch TV.' " He is right; she *can* say that firmly without yelling.

Basically Angry People

If you spend some time observing people's faces, you can learn to read their dominant emotions. Airports are a great place for this! If you watch closely enough, you are likely to observe many facial expressions. Some people look angry even when they seem to be relaxed. Their eyes focus intently, their jaws are set in hard lines, and their lips look tightly pressed.

Many angry people have learned to cover their hurts and tears with a protective coat of armor—aggression. They think the shield will deflect any more hurt from their lives. And in some ways, the shield works. But unfortunately, it makes them unaware of their harshness, of the way in which they hurt others—especially their children.

Angry mothers often yell without even realizing it. And this combination of an angry face and a screaming voice can overwhelm a sensitive child.

Angry moms are often insensitive to the child's painful feelings. Such a lack is not due to a mother's badness, but it is a part of the emotional hardness that has helped her survive the tough times she has had to endure. These callouses may protect the mother, but they prevent her sensitivity to the children she actually loves very much!

Correcting such a problem is no easy task. Begin with admitting to yourself that you have become angry. Look honestly at your face in a mirror. Do you see the telltale expression of anger there? Ask a loving and honest friend. Does she see you as an aggressive, easily-angered woman?

If what you see and hear reflect to you a basic anger, begin breaking those habits. The blueprints for remodeling an angry, bitter personality into one of clear-thinking and love are waiting for you! And they are definitely worth your time and attention.

6

How to Get Control of Yourself

> That woman who is cool and collected, who is master of her countenance, her voice, her actions, and her gestures, will be the mother who is in control of her children, and who is greatly beloved by them.—Old Inscription

Like it or not, mothers set the tone of the home. As a mother, you have probably noticed that when you are in control, the children are much easier to keep under control. But when you are upset for any reason, the children are usually "off the wall." Children are sensitive; they respond dramatically to the emotional pulse of the mother.

We've already discussed what causes mothers to lose control. Now let's look at some positive ways to gain control.

Planning Ahead and Organization

A controlled mother plans ahead and is organized. Remember—you need to be the *master* of the day, rather than the *victim*. It is vital to have a strategy for the day that includes anticipating potential problems and planning how to deal with them.

Problems arise when most of life is a surprise and you are caught

off guard and unprepared. When this happens, you can automatically be thrown out of control until you regroup and sort out the
chaos of the moment.

Rita,* a newly organized mother, tells this story:

I used to just get up and let the day happen. It happened all
right, and most of it was bad. Everyone else was controlling my
life—my children, my husband, my friends. I began to feel used,
abused, and resentful, and decided to make a change. I wanted
to feel that I had some control, even a little, over my life and
time.

To help myself get organized, I began to make lists on little
scraps of paper that I would misplace and lose. Oh well! I felt I
was on the right track. Later on, I bought an organizer, and actually began to enjoy writing down my plans for the day, the
week, the month. It became a game to see how many of the
things I had written down I could actually get done.

Little by little, my family and friends began to have some
respect for my time and plans. I really feel it has been because I
can say I am doing certain other things, and, wonder of wonders,
I am even learning to say, "No!" to foolish requests.

For many people, becoming organized is far from easy—it is
heroic. Kim* wanted very much to keep a neat house, have all the
laundry done up-to-date, prepare nourishing meals, and spend
time with her children. For years she zigzagged. When the house
was clean the laundry piled up, and when the meals were outstanding she had a messy house.

One day in desperation she viewed the small mountain of
laundry, her messy house, and quarrelsome children. She decided
to take charge of her home and family. First she made a list, carefully arranging the jobs to be done. She packed the dirty laundry in six
heavy-duty trash bags and took them to her local laundromat.
While it washed and dried she read to her children and then got
them to help fold and carefully put away their own things.

Next she put a tasty dinner in the oven. While it cooked, she and the children raced through the house picking up and putting away things. Soon the house was in order, the laundry heap had vanished, and a delicious and attractive meal graced the table. Her husband was proud and amazed. But best of all, she knew she could manage the demands of her household—because she learned how to plan, prioritize, and follow through. So can you.

Flexibility

A controlled mother is flexible. Some moms tend to make following a schedule more important than meeting the needs of their children. This rigidity will result in loss of control and, ultimately, in screaming. Life is full of interruptions, emergencies, crises, and urgent happenings. A mother must train herself to go with the flow, even if it means temporarily abandoning her plan or realizing that it goes against the natural inclinations of her personality. It isn't always easy, especially at the start, but the rewards are tremendous.

Although Kate* struggled with flexibility for months, she found it reaped great benefits in her family life.

When my daughter was a toddler, she reached that stage where she wanted to touch everything. She knew what "No!" meant, and she heard it often!

I had great plans for this particular Saturday and needed to leave the house, but my daughter was exerting her very strong will. She reached out to touch something. I said, "No!" but she touched it anyway. I slapped her hand to reaffirm that it was, "No!" This did not deter her, and she touched the object again and again.

I was irritated and perplexed. Should I stay at home and reinforce the behavior pattern she was defying, or should I carry on with my plans? I really felt we were at a crisis point, and that she needed moment by moment consistency. I reluctantly cancelled my plans and stayed home, spending much of the day saying "No!"

I'm so glad I did. Although she was much harder to train in

that area than my other children, the block of time spent in training her paid off. She learned that "No!" meant "No!" and that she
needed to respect property and not touch everything in sight.

While mothers often need to be flexible in terms of changing their
own plans, there is another type of flexibility that will help prevent
screaming: know when to bend the rules and give just a bit. Although children require an equal consistency, they also need to
have special privileges now and then. Knowing when to allow a
shorter practice time or a bit longer TV time can create a bond of
appreciation that will strengthen your love. Your children will realize that you extend consideration to them.

If your child has had an especially tough day at school, is
pestered by a brother or sister, and has a load of homework, it may
be extremely useful to allow him to skip piano practice or doing
dishes for one night. Be careful, though, to make such exceptions a
rarity so the child will not learn to manipulate but rather to accept
the gesture as a gift.

A Sense of Humor

A controlled mother has a sense of humor. The mother who can
laugh at herself, with the children, and at the impossible situations
of life rather than take them too seriously is far ahead on the road
to personal control. Having the wisdom to step back and see the
humor of her situation helped Sharon* gain control:

It was the night of the school Christmas Pageant and the first
program the older two had ever been in. At that time, I had a
four-year-old girl, a three-year-old girl, and a baby of nine
months. My husband was gone, and the children were constantly at each other. Besides that, so many little things went wrong.
Socks to wear with dresses were missing, the children had each
spilled food all over themselves and their clothes, hair was extra
unruly, and I was exhausted with the ordeal of getting them
ready and out the door. When I discovered the car keys were

missing, I felt frustration plus! Believe me, I was literally ready to tear my hair out.

Suddenly I realized how funny the whole situation was! I was in the middle of a situation comedy that no one would ever see but me! I sat down in the middle of the floor and began to laugh. I laughed so hard the tears came. My children didn't know what to think. They sat down on the floor with me and put their arms around me. But you know what? We found the keys—under a pillow of all places—and just barely managed to get to the program in time.

Balance

A controlled mother strives to keep balance in her life. A mother is often frustrated and weary at the end of the day—not only because of her work load but because she has not had time to pursue activities that are important to her personal growth and development. Since the stimulation of variety dispels boredom and fatigue, change can give fulfillment to the inner being while releasing frustration and increasing enthusiasm.

You may feel like each day becomes a juggling act. You have to balance commitment to your husband, your children, your home, and your work, and yet have some time to pursue special projects, compelling interests, and friendships. Whew! What a task!

But achieving balance can change your attitude toward your children. It did for Carol.*

I almost went crazy being a mother. I had three children in five years and was under a daily load of laundry, dishes, a house strewn with paraphernalia, and sticky fingerprints decorating my walls. I had been an art designer and longed to spend time alone in what had once been my studio but was now a catch-all room! I was so frustrated with never having time for my art that I began to wish I'd never had children. Then I would feel guilty and miserable.

For a while I assumed I was the only mother who had ever felt trapped. I confided my feelings to another mother of three. She felt the same way. We thought of a plan to babysit twice a week for each other for a half day. We've been doing it now for almost a year. Having that time alone to pursue my art work has made all the difference to me and my children. I can now enjoy them, knowing I'll have some well-earned time for myself.

Other helpful suggestions for finding your balance in life may occur to you. We suggest learning to say "No!" to tasks you may be asked (and even *wish*) to do. When your children are more independent you can take on additional jobs.

We sometimes wonder why mothers don't think about hiring a babysitter when they are at home. An older child may love to babysit while you do something you'd like or even take a nap! It costs very little, helps a young person earn a little money, and offers a fresh opportunity for your children to expand their relationships.

Finally, learning that "deep" cleaning and some other household tasks can wait for a time (even several years!) can relieve your mind. If you are an orderly person, it may be just as hard for you to let certain jobs go undone as it is for the disorganized mothers to learn to plan and prioritize. But try it. It could help you find your balance.

A Positive Attitude

A controlled mother has a positive attitude. The eminent psychologist William James said, "The greatest discovery of my generation is that you can change your circumstances by changing your attitudes of mind." Here is a classic illustration of a mother with a positive attitude:

Great, great grandmother, on a winter's day,
milked the cows and fed them hay,
slopped the hogs, saddled the mule,
then got the children off to school,

did a washing, mopped the floors,
washed the windows, and did some chores;
cooked a dish of home-dried fruit,
pressed her husband's Sunday suit.
Swept the parlor, made the bed,
baked a dozen loaves of bread,
split some firewood, and then lugged in
enough to fill the kitchen bin;
cleaned the lamps and put in oil,
stewed some apples she thought would spoil;
churned the butter, baked a cake,
then exclaimed, "For heaven's sake,
the calves have got out of the pen"—
went out and chased them in again.

Gathered the eggs and locked the stable,
back to the house and set the table,
cooked a supper that was delicious,
and afterward washed up all the dishes,
fed the cat and sprinkled the clothes,
mended a basketful of hose;
then opened the organ and began to play,
"When You Come to the End of a Perfect Day."
—Author Unknown

This great lady was in control of herself and her life largely because of an incredibly positive attitude toward her responsibilities.

If you happen to be a more critical person, you may find it difficult to change your attitude. Don't expect an immediate transformation—just try to add some hopeful comments in the midst of any criticism you feel you need to state. Solving problems together, correcting mistakes with kindness, and forgiving each other can restore hope to your child and strengthen the love between you.

It is not easy to plan ahead, to be flexible, to have a sense of humor when frustrated, to keep a balanced life, and to have a positive attitude. But each is a worthy and attainable goal for the mother who longs to stop screaming and get control of herself. Each is possible to attain most of the time if you have the courage to replace screaming with organization, flexibility, humor, balance, and a positive attitude.

Ralph Waldo Emerson said, "That which we persist in doing becomes easier for us to do; not that the nature of the thing itself is changed, but that our power to do is increased."

A Prescription for Change

A controlled mother has a prescription for change. You mothers who scream realize, of course, that you do it for a good reason. We have reviewed many of those causes in chapter two and why it's so hard to stop in chapter five. Now we'd like to offer you some clear and proven steps that will enable you to change.

Motivation
Breaking any habit is so much trouble that one must truly want to do it. Few habits are harder to break than screaming. Some ideas that may motivate you are:

- happier, better adjusted children;
- a desire to be a better mother;
- wishing to enjoy good feelings rather than the shame or remorse you experience after yelling;
- the approval of your spouse, parents, or friends because of your changing;
- confidence that you can learn better, more successful parenting skills.

Permission to change
This idea may sound foolish at first but think about it. Chances are you yell because you were taught to yell—by your mother, by accidentally discovering it worked, or by some other means. To begin to change, then, you must believe it's okay and that you can find better methods.

It's a good idea to discuss your ideas for changing with someone else. A person who has found ways of handling children without screaming is one of your best allies.

Decide firmly to change

How often we think about breaking a habit. Do these sound familiar? *I* ought *to go on a diet!* Or, *I really* should *learn to control my spending.* And, *I* need *to organize my time better.* All of these words (*ought, should,* and *need*) are emphatic and indicate intentions to change. But we can assure you that change will not happen automatically.

We recommend that you think clearly and emphatically, something like this: "I know my screaming does more damage than good. I *choose* to stop screaming, and I *will* begin to break that habit today." It takes a definite decision and commitment to effect change.

Formulate a plan

Outline a goal that is *possible* for you to reach. Each day, can you scream one time less than usual? On at least one occasion when you would normally yell, make yourself avoid doing so. Learn to recognize the early warning signs of an emotional storm. Before that storm bursts, put your feelings into words. "I feel *anxious* that I may be unable to handle this problem." Or, "I am just *furious* because you broke that special cup!" Thinking about your emotions will begin to put you in control of them—instead of allowing them to take charge of you.

Next think about what really has upset you so much. On the surface, of course, it's something your child has said or done—or *not* done! But when you consider a situation even a bit more, you will often discover some underlying memory or a deep fear of losing parental authority. We have even known mothers whose children acted very much like their grandparents. One mother faintly heard her father's domineering voice in her daughter's bossy back-talk.

Knowing how you feel and why you feel that way will enable you to make a pivotal decision. "What will I do about this situation that will really cure it?" You may take time out in order to plan the

answer carefully. Waiting for your action is a very useful part of the
disciplinary response children need. They can ponder their misbehavior and become a bit anxious. Being uncomfortable inside
may help them decide to overcome problem habits!

Find some help

To change any habit we need a friend to remind us when we fall into
the old patterns and to encourage us when the going gets rough.
Find that special person (perhaps your own child) and ask her if she
will be available to you for several weeks. When you are about to
resort to screaming, run to the phone and call for help. If you fail to
reach your goals for a day or more, tell her you need encouragement. Many times a friend you need desperately is not there when
you call, but even the act of trying can give you the time to regain
your control.

   We want to remind you that God is always on call! Don't forget
to contact Him for the patience and wisdom you will need. One
way to communicate with Him is to imagine His presence near you.
After you ask for help, listen! You may be amazed, not at hearing a
physical voice, but at the unique ideas that pop into your mind.

Follow through

The best plans in the world will fall flat unless you put them to
work. People often say, "I really tried that idea but it didn't work."
With some mental exploring, they often discover that they unwittingly expected it to work just by talking about it. *You* must work
the plan day after day, even when it seems unsuccessful. Bad habits
take time to develop, and changes also take time. You may never
know how close to success you were because you gave up just short
of the finish line. It's at such a point of discouragement when your
friend can be of the most value.

Professional Help

As we have already said, there are some reasons for screaming that
have physical bases. Be sure to see your doctor on a regular basis
and keep your body healthy.

Equally common are some psychological, emotional, and even spiritual "blind spots" that may prevent your seeing issues clearly. You may have convinced yourself that screaming is okay since it seems to work. Possibly you are unable to see how it is angering or scaring your child.

We urge you to have a personal and a family checkup. A good family counselor can see issues more clearly and objectively than you who are so close to them. That counsel can be invaluable. Often only a few visits can get you past the pressure points to a place where you can develop and carry out your new methods of discipline *and* build a loving relationship at the same time.

We know you can do it!

7

Corralling Your Kids

Happy, smiling faces,
Busy fingers,
Helping hands.
The music of their laughter,
The dancing of their feet.
Good times together
Without tiresome whining
Or ugly pouting.
All who look nod and smile . . .
The beauty of the well behaved.

Every mother's dream is to speak softly and get a cheerful, obedient response from attentive, cooperative children. An *impossible dream*? No, but it requires that the mother behave as the controlled, firm, loving, fair, consistent authority figure who *chooses* not to scream. There is a way to make this dream become your reality.

"Velvet over steel" is a three-word picture of the mother who is fun, loving, soft, gentle, yet exudes strength and control. The undergirding of strength and control allows her to be fun-loving with her children and even permits her to act silly. She can do it because she is still in control of herself and in control of her children. She knows it, and they know it!

Steel gives strength and meaning to each word the mother speaks. Steel doesn't need to scream, "I am strong. Please believe me, I really am strong!" Steel *is* strong. Steel can be a raised eyebrow, a look on a mother's face, a glance across a room, or a meeting of eyes that penetrates the heart of an understanding child.

Velvet is what every mother wants to be, the part of the mother's personality she wants to reveal. The undergirding of steel makes it possible.

The velvet-over-steel mother controls her children in three very positive ways. Let's discuss them.

Say What You Mean, and Mean What You Say

The velvet-over-steel mother says what she means and means what she says—all of the time. This requires thinking, planning, and following through with confidence, and above all, consistency. A mother must learn to be consistent, even when she is tired, overcommitted, and under excessive stress. A mother can choose to discipline herself to be consistent regardless of what is going on (or not going on) in her life. Consistency with the children will reap rewards that will help the rest of life to fall into proper perspective.

When you sense the breaking point coming, rather than screaming, take time to be silent and think. Think about the consequences of what you are going to say and do so you can be a mother without regrets.

Grocery stores are an inevitable problem for mothers of young children. This mother unfortunately said something she really did not mean.

I was busy, running late, had to fix dinner, and had an evening class to attend. Time was of the essence. My five-year-old was cranky and uncooperative. I asked him to get a box of cereal for himself. He loudly snapped, "No, I won't." Other shoppers heard his overly loud remark as they wheeled their carts by. I knew I had to do something, but what? If I spanked him, he would just get louder. I felt myself getting more angry as well as embarrassed. Out of sheer frustration, I screamed, "I'm NEVER bringing you here again!"

How fortunate for this five-year-old! He never wanted to go to the boring grocery store in the first place. But what will the mother do? Has she really disciplined her son, or has she punished herself? For the next few years, is she really only going to go to the grocery store when her son is in school or when she has someone else to watch him? She has trapped herself into a very difficult situation by not taking the time to assess her options and the consequences for both herself and her son before taking action.

While she is thinking and planning what course of action to take, a mother's silence can be momentarily misunderstood by the child and interpreted as "getting by" with the unacceptable behavior. But in time the child will learn to have a healthy respect for mother's silence.

For example, several years ago, Pat entered the house with her fifth-grade daughter, was going through the mail, and became un-usually silent. Her eighth-grade son's grades had come and were not in keeping with his ability, nor were they at the level of previous years. She was thinking about how to handle the situation before approaching him.

Her daughter sensed the unnatural silence, and asked, "Mom, have I done anything wrong?"

Pat responded, "No, why do you ask?"

"Well," her daughter said, "You are being very, very quiet, and you have that real serious look on your face—the one you get when one of us has done something."

Pat immediately reassured her daughter, and for the first time began to be consciously aware not only of the wisdom of silence in discipline, but also of the power of silence in discipline.

Practicing the art of silence is one of the most difficult disciplines in this world, at least for many of us! That is why we have written about learning and using self-control. If you will master this skill and use it to stay quiet instead of impulsively screaming out your

rage and demands, you may transform your family life. Once you
have conquered the screaming habit, replace it with self-control,
silence, and thoughtfulness. Then you will know what you mean to
say, and you can say what you really mean.

Probably the most important benefit to a mother who means what
she says, and says what she means is that her child is given a firm foun-
dation of trust and confidence. The child knows that he or she can
count on what the mother says because she means it. The child doesn't
need to argue and whine, because the mother means what she says
the first time. Arguing and whining are largely eliminated when the
mother is confident that her decisions are fair and right. She cannot
be worn down or manipulated because she is secure and the child can
trust her. She means every word she says, whether it is a treat
promised or a disciplinary action. The mother will not forget or
change her mind when she cools down or when other things interfere.
Because his world is predictable, the child feels secure and gains self-
esteem. Remember that predictability is one of the most vital emotional needs of every child.

State the Desired Behavior and Results Ahead of Time

A mother needs to state the desired behavior ahead of time and
what the positive and negative consequences will be. The mother
who sets limits ahead of time, explains what is expected, what the
reward of obedience will be, and what the result of disobedience
will be, can never be labeled as "unfair." Why? The choice to obey
or disobey becomes the choice of the child.

For example, let's take another look at the grocery store scene.

> I was busy, running late, had to fix dinner, and had an evening
> class to attend. Time was of the essence. My five-year-old was
> cranky and uncooperative. I asked him to get a box of cereal. He
> loudly snapped, "No, I won't."

The mother who follows this principle would look very seriously and sternly at her son, and say in a soft, but firm voice, "You know what to do in this grocery store. We went over what to do, and you told me all the right things. You need to do them each and every time we are here. Because you chose not to do the right things and help me, you will not get your special grocery store treat today. Not only will you not get your special treat, but when we get home, you may not go to Jimmy's house to play ball." The little boy would begin to sniffle.

"I'm very sorry that you did not choose to obey, and I hope that this will help you to remember how to help Mommy the next time we come to the store."

Unlike the mother in the first sequence, this mother knows that there will be many, many grocery store trips with her son. He simply must learn to cooperate or suffer the consequences. In the past, she has reviewed the grocery store standards of behavior with her son. He will be disciplined for his unacceptable behavior in two ways. He will lose out on the positive reward of a grocery store treat that he was to enjoy for being helpful during a rather boring time for him. He will also miss playing ball with his good friend Jimmy, something he really wanted to do. This loss of privileges will help him to remember to behave the next time he goes to the grocery store with his mother.

This loving mother has set a behavior standard of grocery store cooperation which she feels is wise and correct. The boy knew what was expected ahead of time and had verbalized the behavior so that the mother was certain he understood. He had also been given the incentive of a "grocery store treat"—the positive reward. He had been told that if he did not "help in the grocery store," he would not be able to go to Jimmy's house to play ball—the negative consequence. The boy chose to misbehave. The consequence of his behavior is no surprise to him. The mother did not respond from anger or embarrassment but simply followed through with a previously arranged agreement.

Stating the desired behavior ahead of time, and what the positive and negative consequences will be, works with teenagers as well. Let's follow up the story of Pat's son's grades.

I was stunned at his first quarter eighth-grade marks. He had always been an excellent student. Frankly, there had never been a need to discuss consequences of poor grades until this time. I first told my son I wanted to talk with him after dinner. (I don't believe that mealtime should be destroyed with unpleasant conversation, and the matter didn't involve his sister, anyway.) He said, "Sure," but wondered why. I told him to be prepared to discuss his report card, knowing that waiting for discipline can enhance its effectiveness by allowing the child to think about the issue.

After dinner I showed him the grades and asked for his explanation. He told me he hadn't studied like he should have, missed turning in some assignments, and had generally not applied himself. I asked what he planned to do in the next quarter. He told me that he would study harder, turn in assignments, and apply himself.

All that sounded good, but being a firm believer in positive and negative consequences, I needed to do more. I asked him if he liked attending the private school he was at. He did. I asked him if he wanted to continue there. He did. I told him that if his grades improved, his father and I would continue paying the tuition that enabled him to attend this private school (the positive consequence), but that if his grades did not improve, then he would forfeit the right to attend the school and be placed elsewhere (the negative consequence).

My son knew I meant what I said and that the choice was his—to do better and remain in the school or save his parents a lot of expense and be placed elsewhere. His grades improved steadily, he stayed in the school, graduated with honors, and we never had such a talk regarding grades again.

Balancing positive and negative consequences is a continual challenge for the mother because what is positive and negative for a child varies from age to age and stage to stage. A mother must know what is important to the child and will often be surprised by how simple the positive really can be.

Tammy,* the mother of a second-grader, was having a struggle getting her little girl to assume simple responsibilities around the house. She had "tried everything," and "nothing worked." We spoke casually with the little girl and found out that "the best thing of all is going to the donut shop on Saturday mornings!" Her mother had never realized that this meant so much to the little girl. Encouraging the child with a visit to the donut shop was just the motivation the little girl needed to complete her chores.

As children grow in their ability to understand a reason, include them in establishing rules for family living. They are often helpful in deciding on the positive and negative consequences as well. After all, who should know better than the child what will be most meaningful to him or her in learning important lessons?

One family set up a weekly family council. In a friendly, businesslike fashion, they discussed all the concerns of each family member—what they needed, special privileges certain activities would require, who had a quarrel against whom, and whose household jobs were especially well done (or needed more attention). Their communications system worked so well they discovered that no one needed to scream any more. Eventually this family used their council time to express their appreciation and respect and just to have fun together.

Make a Conscious Choice to Enjoy Your Children

The velvet-over-steel mother makes a conscious choice to *enjoy* her children. Since the child-rearing path is strewn with so many hazards, mothers need to determine to enjoy their children rather than to grimly accept the current stage (the "I can't wait till it's over syndrome").

A very wise mother of eight once said, "Your child has the right to be the age he or she is for 365 days, just as you have the right to be the age you are for 365 days." Accepting this as fair, mothers might just as well decide to pass the year in enjoyment rather than with seething frustration that erupts with frequent bouts of screaming.

Making this philosophy work demands that you learn something about the capabilities of children at a particular age. Observe the children of relatives and friends and talk with those parents. Watch your own child and see what she is able to do by herself. Remember, each child is unique so no two will fit the same capacity, but you can collect some guidelines that will enable you to be more fair.

This little motto has helped Grace discover how to enjoy her children: "Explore—before you expect!" As you encourage, observe, listen, and teach, you will not only enjoy, but, we believe, become excited as you watch your children develop!

In an ancient Chinese alphabet, the characters used to describe "crisis" are interpreted in English as "dangerous opportunity." That is exactly what every discipline situation is—a dangerous opportunity. *If* the mother exercises self-control and chooses to be fair, firm, loving, and consistent, the crisis situation becomes an exciting opportunity to build character and self-esteem in her children and to enhance her loving relationship with her children built on mutual love and respect. *If*, however, the mother does not exercise self-control but indulges in screaming, then she faces the dangers of reaping the harvest we have discussed.

A mother can do several specific things to increase her enjoyment of her children:

Listen to your children—really listen to their stories and ask questions that show interest, rather than questions that are critical or skeptical. Enjoy their stories, don't just tolerate them. Look at them as they talk and stop whatever you are doing so they know you are interested.

Spend time with your children doing the things that are important to them at their age and stage. If you ask with genuine caring, they will be glad to tell you, and share themselves with you. No other task is as important as this. Children *can't* wait!

Talk with them as very important persons, rather than as people who never remember to pick up clothes or take out the garbage. Try saying, "You are a neat person, and I doubt you can feel very good when you let yourself get by with a careless job!"

Laugh with them. Children are wonderful. The freshness of their stories, their creativity, and their honesty (although appalling at times!) cannot fail to make a mother laugh rather than grit her teeth or clench her jaws—*if* she chooses laughter. Laugh *with* them, and be cautious to avoid seeming to laugh *at* them.

As part of a research project several years ago, we asked approximately fifty junior-high girls, "What will you do when you are a mother?" They were encouraged to be honest and not put their names on their papers. There was no discussion of the question. Their answers reveal the importance of listening, talking, laughing, and spending time together.

I won't scream at my children. I will have talks with them and explain why it isn't right to do bad things. If they don't learn by these talks, I will discipline them. I will tell them I love them. If they have problems at school or with friends, I will ask them if they want to talk about it. If they don't want to talk about their problems, I will tell them I care about them and their problems. Then I will sit and talk with them and try to help them with their problems.

I think when I'm a mother, I will discipline my children enough so they won't be spoiled, but not a lot so they will hate me. We'll go together to parks and to ice cream parlors and things like that. I'll live in a cozy house, and once in a while, especially when it's raining, have a fire and pop popcorn. I think when I'm a mother, I'm going to laugh and have fun with my children.

For this moment in time, you are the mother. You are the one who is building the museum of memories. Mothers make mistakes,

and that's okay. If children feel loved and supported in an atmos-
phere of enjoyment, they will forgive, accept, and enjoy mothers to
the same degree that mothers forgive, accept, and enjoy them.
Then their memories will be pleasant, and so will yours.

Grace reminisces:

> It was on a vacation that I discovered that I could enjoy my
> children. My husband and I were frankly a bit bored. In fact he
> had fallen asleep on a sunny afternoon in our hotel room. Ac-
> cidentally, I focused on the faint but merry laughter pealing from
> the next room. It was our children! No boredom in their room.
> As quietly as possible, I slipped into their room and joined their
> fun. Their comments and insights were hilariously funny. I felt
> really favored when they allowed me to laugh with them and
> especially important when they laughed at my efforts to be
> humorous. That event became a landmark in my relationship
> with my children. By rediscovering the enjoyment of joking and
> laughing together, we became a team—not opposing forces.

Develop a Ceremony for Change

Jill* had scolded and yelled at her son, Dan, for years. Actually she
was anxiety-ridden over his habit of daydreaming and procrastina-
tion. He was late to meals, often forgot to care for his pets, and
seemed unaware of time deadlines.

One day an article she read made Jill's mothering take a brand
new course. She suddenly understood that her nagging and screaming had been pushing her son away. He loved her but could not bear
her disapproving lectures and angry looks. The more she yelled, the
further he withdrew. There was real danger of out-and-out rebellion. Furthermore, in her concern over Dan's few (but irritating!)
problems, Jill had long since forgotten to compliment Dan on his
sense of humor, his kindness and generosity to others, and his basic
good judgment.

After considerable thought, Jill found a convenient time to talk
privately with Dan. For the first time he could recall in his thirteen

years, she solemnly admitted she had been wrong. She listed all the specifics of her mistakes and clearly apologized for the hurts they had inflicted on his developing personality.

Dan hastily tried to reassure his mother. He reminded her that she was right about his procrastinating and that he needed her reminders. Jill, however, held fast. She was tempted to accept his excuses for her, but she knew too well that she had been disastrously wrong in her methods. She thanked him for his characteristic comfort but held to her apology.

Next Jill listed for Dan all the outstanding traits she had taken for granted in him. And she apologized again for her failure to express to him how much those qualities meant to her. Jill's agenda led her to the best part of her ceremony. Not only did she ask Dan to forgive her, but she sought *his* help in making *her* changes. What a reversal of roles! And it was long overdue. Jill explained her well-ordered plan for change, but she knew her habits were deeply ingrained. She would need Dan to remind her when she slipped back into her old habits. And when he at times forgot his responsibilities, she would need him to tell her when he would do them so she could avoid the screaming.

Dan was quietly overjoyed. He assured his mom that he would work on his end of things and he'd be glad to remind her when she slipped. They both held to their agreement. Of course they both fell into old habits at times, but their ceremonious commitment to change and their deep love for each other held them steady. They made it! And so can you.

The whole purpose of gaining control over your children is to teach them eventual self-control. You would have had a much easier time as a mother who rarely screamed if you had mastered self-control years ago. What a wonderful opportunity you now have to break the habits of generations! You *can* acquire self-control. By your example as well as your careful teaching, you can help your children master this task and build a priceless quality into their lives.

8

The Key to Healing

From our research and experience, one truth predominates: The art of forgiveness is the secret of a contented life. But tragically, there are many mothers who have never considered the need to forgive either themselves, their children, or others for real and/or imagined offenses. Here's what one mother said:

> I hate to admit this, but most of motherhood has been disappointing for me. Instead of being fun and rewarding, I have more days when I feel trapped by the financial and time restraints my three children cause. I sometimes feel cheated that I am giving the best years of my life to three children who don't want to listen to me most of the time, and are eager to disobey. Then I feel like an utter failure and wonder what I've done so wrong that I can even think such terrible thoughts!

No mother wants to feel trapped, caged, imprisoned. Yet harboring unforgiveness will gradually turn a life into a strong fortress of pain built with the iron bars of hurt, anger, and resentment, and fortified with cross bars of guilt and bitterness.

Dr. Foster Cline, a psychiatrist who has studied troubled people extensively, said, "Good mental health depends on living in a constant state of forgiveness!" We would add, "and so does a good mother-child relationship."

There is freedom in forgiveness. Freedom, stability, and self-control in life always accompany forgiveness. A mother must take two steps before she can experience the healing and freedom of forgiveness. What are they?

Forgive Yourself

A mother's fantasy is to smile at her children as she speaks kind words softly and tenderly, breaking frequently into bubbly laughter. Too often, threats and screams become a mother's reality instead. Julia,* whose youngest is now in college, admitted,

> My screaming caused me to feel so guilty. I remember thinking many times during those early years of motherhood, "What am I doing to these children?" I would go to bed with guilt weighing heavily on me, and I can recall crying out to God, "Why did You give me these children? I am just not a good mother!"

Oversensitive mothers become quickly disappointed because they have not measured up to their own expectations. Guilt grinds away in their emotions and thought processes, and they are left with a battered remnant of self-worth. Kari* shared how she felt:

> I have a problem. I berate myself and tell myself after each screaming fit that my children will stop loving me if I ever do it again. That causes me to live in a continual state of anxiety and agitation. Of course, I scream again, berate myself, and so it goes.

It is so important to understand the difference between real and false guilt. You *are* guilty if you have done wrong or have broken the laws of society or the rules of living lovingly. If you have hurt your child physically or emotionally, you *are* guilty. You certainly did not intend to, and so you feel awful about it. That terrible feeling can motivate you to begin to change. A major factor in that change is learning how to forgive yourself and really begin to love yourself.

False guilt, by contrast, is a feeling based on misinformation—not facts. Because of habits that are rooted in childhood experiences and family practices and beliefs, you may feel that you have done wrong. Were you to see anyone else doing a similar act, however, you would not feel they were at fault. If you were to name a law or principle that you had broken, you would have difficulty defining it.

For example, a teenager once told Grace that she felt extremely guilty because at the tender age of three, she had been unable to stop her stepfather from beating her mother. She even tried repeatedly to harm herself in an attempt to punish herself for being bad.

Many people cannot seem to find forgiveness because they are, in fact, not guilty. It is correct information that removes false guilt. So, in reading further, be careful to define which type of guilt you feel. Do not rationalize and make genuine guilt seem faultless, and do not berate yourself for imagined wrongdoing. If you aren't certain, ask a friend, clergy, or counselor because honesty is essential in this process of forgiving.

Some mothers have specific reasons for their feelings of guilt:

Yes, I feel guilty about my children, because I am guilty. I had already nearly raised three children, when I divorced, remarried, and—to my horror—two more children arrived on the scene. About this time my second husband took off, and I was left with two young children to support by myself at this stage of my life. Yes, I am angry—angry that I married another bum, that I was foolish enough to have the children, that I have no money, and that I have to work full-time again to eke out a living for the three of us. I guess I retaliate by working the "graveyard" shift, although I don't have to. In that way I see my children as little as possible, since they're usually in day care or with assorted babysitters. When I am with them, I often need to sleep. If they don't let me sleep, I really scream at them, reminding them if I don't get my sleep, I'll lose my job, and then where will we all be? My children, now ages six and nine, are having terrible problems at school. Both are failing academically and socially. The older one acts out his anger, and the younger one withdraws into his own fantasy world. My life is a mess!

This mother's confession screams of her own inner anguish—her helplessness, loneliness, remorse, and daily lashing out at the children who symbolize her own life pattern of disillusionment. She feels guilty, and she *is* guilty. The good news for her (and others like her) is that she can change. By forgiving herself, she can regain her self-respect. By forgiving her husband, "the Bum," she will no longer resent his traits in the children. Through these steps of forgiveness, she will be able to love herself and her children with new depth.

Forgiving ourselves is the first step. Once we accomplish this, we are able to take the second.

Forgive Others

Some of the mothers in our interviews have reasons not to forgive—legitimate reasons. They have been abandoned, rejected, abused, and wronged in a variety of ways. They have lived with enormous hurt and pain, some for many years. Perhaps you, too, have good reasons, understandable reasons, for not forgiving your children, spouse, parent, or significant others in your life. Staying angry seems to offer protection against further hurts.

However, you must forgive if you want harmony in your home. The price tag for unforgiveness is too high. Festering hurt leads to anger, resentment, bitterness, and depression. If any of these are not admitted and dealt with, they will begin to affect your relationship with those around you, including your children, causing physical as well as emotional problems.

Many mothers erroneously think that if they bury the hurts and the pain, they will mysteriously disappear in time. Nothing could be further from the truth. Time does *not* heal all wounds. In fact, if the wounds of life are repressed or suppressed in the hope of getting rid of them, the opposite will happen. These wounds will grow until at last they emerge with far greater intensity and potential for destruction than they initially had. Hannah More, an English author of the 1700's, understood this. She said, "A person will find it cheaper to pardon than to resent. Forgiveness saves the expense of anger, the cost of hatred, the waste of spirits."

It is also vital to understand that the act of forgiving another, whoever it might be, is really more for the benefit of the one doing the forgiving than for the one who needs to be forgiven. Forgiveness enables us to be whole and in control of life and our reactions to circumstances. When unpleasant situations come up that cause hurt and anger, we can immediately choose to forgive. By that supremely powerful act of the will—making the choice to forgive—we come to be in charge of our lives. It is through exercising self-control that we learn to forgive.

To experience healing through forgiveness of others, a mother needs to take action. Here are a few steps you can take:

Release the other person by an act of the will.
Pat writes from her own experience:

> I know all too well what it is like to endure stabs of humiliation, and receive the mortal wound of rejection. Over a period of time, the pain gradually turned into anger, which I denied even to myself. I can recall mornings waking up angry, with rage fomenting inside, not really aware of where it had come from or why.
>
> As I went through each day, something or somebody would often remind me of a particular hurt. I would mentally take the incident out of my memory bank, go over every single detail, remember each word and action, and relive my feelings of pain and helplessness. All this was done with a maximum amount of self-pity, I assure you.
>
> Although I was consumed with my problem, endlessly going over what I wish I'd have said and done at different times, I

longed to run away from my angry and destructive thoughts. But where could I go?

At this precise time, when I felt there was no hope, and no way of escape, I believe God showed me that the answer to my restless anxiety, grieving pain, and unrelenting anger was forgiveness. I began my arduous journey into forgiveness by first realizing it didn't matter if I were right, and the other person (or people) wrong. I had to forgive by an act of my will and make a conscious choice to forgive.

I began to repeat, "By an act of my will, I choose to forgive _____." Each time during the day and night a hurting episode flashed through my mind, I would think, "By an act of my will, I choose to forgive_____ for doing (or not doing), saying (or not saying) that to me." Complete forgiveness did not come quickly for me. Over and over again, I had to choose to forgive the person (people) for specific acts.

Slowly, the process of continually choosing to forgive began to work changes in my heart and life. I became calmer on the inside. A change of attitude followed, and I became more positive. I also began to feel much better about myself—stronger, more in control, with a greater sense of worth and joy. All this was a surprise! I had no idea the act of forgiving was so powerful. Now I can tell you that, at least for me, there is no adequate way to overestimate the strength, healing, and freedom of forgiveness.

Accept others as they are and release them from the responsibility of meeting your needs.
Diane* shared this story with us:

I've learned a little about forgiveness. I grew up expecting to marry a man who would take care of me in the style I grew up with, and make me happy for the rest of my life. I married when I was young. Because of my father's position, we had been affluent. My husband had no money, and I encouraged him to go to work for my father. My father died several years later, and the business went steadily downhill. "How could my husband do that to me, to the children?" I wondered constantly. "How dare he lose the position, prestige, and money that my father had and that I had enjoyed and expected?"

I became depressed and blamed my husband for everything that had happened to us. I also let him know that he was responsible for my happiness, or lack of it, as well as everything else.

Years later I came to grips with the fact that I never should have pressured him to go to work for my father. He was ill suited for the business from the start. Slowly, I forgave myself for that initial blunder and forgave him for not being like my father. I also recently have begun to realize that my husband is not responsible for my happiness; no one is. That comes from within me. It's a whole new approach for me to accept responsibility for my happiness, rather than blaming my husband. But I'm learning.

This story reinforces the fact that it is only as we learn to accept ourselves that we can honestly accept others. When we learn to take responsibility not only for our actions but also for our feelings, we will be able to practice acceptance of ourselves and others.

View others as tools of growth in life.
This story tells how three bites of jello spelled disaster for a family, but eventually resulted in forgiveness, healing, and growth:

It was the evening of my husband's birthday. We had been married for a year and were having a family dinner with my husband's children. We have a rule at our home. I serve small portions of everything, and if a child wants seconds, that's fine, but the child must finish what is on the plate. It was a rule we made as a family, and the children know it well.

My eleven-year-old stepdaughter asked for seconds on jello, but in a few moments decided she didn't want to finish. Her father told her she must finish it because she had asked for it. She vehemently said "No!" Again her father explained the rule, and she still refused. He tried to reason with her, stressing the importance of following through. Still she refused. At that point, because of her poor attitude, he told her she would stay at the table until she finished. There were three small bites of jello left on her plate.

Forty minutes later, she was still sitting at the table all alone. I had cleaned up, sat down, and told her how much easier it would be just to finish the three bites. She looked at me and said in a venomous voice, "I am not finishing the jello!"

At that point, I told her to go to her room. She said, "I am not going to do that." I pulled her chair out, took her by the arm, and maneuvered her through the kitchen. She began to resist strenuously and screamed at me, "Don't do that! You're not my mother!"

I had given so much and felt I had a good relationship. That remark took the stuffing out of me—all the zest and good feeling left. I called my husband and told him what had transpired. He told his daughter to go to her room immediately and never speak that way to me again.

She started screaming and crying that she hated all of us, stomped up to her bedroom, and slammed the door. I also went to my room to get away from everybody. I could hear her screaming at her father, saying things like, "I hate you because you never take my side. You're all unfair to me."

That did it. I went to her room, and said, "Young lady, you are 100% wrong. I never have and I never will ask anything that isn't fair. You children helped us make the rule about seconds, and you broke that rule tonight. Instead of screaming at everybody and thinking how persecuted you are, take time to think that you did the wrong thing. That's all I have to say." I went to my room.

She did not speak to me the next day. Unknown to me, my husband had told her, "When you come home from school, do your homework, think about all that took place, and discuss your thoughts with me."

The next morning she came up to the sink and said, "You probably won't forgive me, but I want to apologize for my behavior. I was wrong. I know we make the rules and need to abide by them. I'm sorry, and I hope that you will accept my apology." All this was said with increasing tears.

I looked at her for a few minutes before speaking and then said, "If your apology is sincere, I will forgive you." Through her tears she nodded, "Yes," and put her arms around me. I responded with a hug.

Although it was settled for the moment, I felt a serious breech had taken place. At a later time, I talked with her and told her, "It must never happen again. We are a family that discusses things. If we make a rule, we abide by that rule. If we think the rule is not fair, we must discuss it together." I had forgiven her, but it took me several months to feel like I would want to trust her again.

Two years have passed since then. We have never had another problem like that, and my relationship with my stepdaughter has grown deeper and stronger.

As is true in so many situations, the real issue was not the obvious one—the eating of three bites of jello. It was a power struggle to see whether the child could effectively manipulate the new environment, which included her father, stepmother, and a rule established by all of them.

Making an issue out of eating three bites of jello seems ridiculous on the surface. However, an important child-rearing principle is at stake: "Say what you mean, and mean what you say" (refer to chapter seven for details). The daughter was testing both the father and stepmother to see what would happen. This father and stepmother stood united, and the child learned that the parents were a team. They meant what they said when they said it, regardless of her reactions. No wonder this problem never occurred again.

The daughter needed to apologize to the stricken stepmother, and with heroic effort she did. The stepmother likewise had some apologizing to do, and she needed to forgive the daughter for the piercing verbal blow she had received. Left unforgiven, the barbs and ugliness between the stepmother and daughter might have continued and resulted in a permanent breech that would have left all the family members resentful, bitter victims.

Forgiveness is a difficult and lengthy process. However, do not be discouraged. Forgiveness is so essential to living together in harmony it is worth every bit of time and effort!

Make reconciliation with those estranged.
Grace writes,

> The screaming that so estranged my mother and me is a tragic collection of childhood memories. It took years to overcome the broken self-esteem and to build respect and warmth. I recall wanting desperately to be able to hug my mother, and I couldn't. I wanted her approval but felt I merited neither that nor her love. What a predicament!
>
> During the pregnancy of my second child, Mother suffered a severe stroke and died at only sixty-three. My son never knew her. Mournfully, I followed my mother's coffin down the long aisle of the church after the funeral. Each member of my family was thinking their own silent thoughts, but I experienced a strangely comforting idea. "The next time I see her, we will at last understand each other!" But that healing did not need to wait until I joined my mother in heaven. I am delighted to share with you how beautifully it did come about.
>
> During a period of training in my psychiatric education, students were learning to use a variety of techniques. One of these was called "The Empty Chair." In this concept, the therapist asks the patient, who has an unresolved problem with another person, to draw on his imagination. By pretending that person is sitting in the empty chair, he or she says to that person whatever needs to be said or asked. Then the person moves to the empty chair, imagines he or she is the other person, and makes the appropriate reply.
>
> It was in learning this concept of counseling that I chose to work on my still unresolved problem with Mother. Quietly and tearfully, I poured out all the childish pain, yearning, and confusion that had been locked away for so many years. When I

moved to Mother's chair and began to consider how she would have responded, I was amazed at the emotions and ideas that flooded my consciousness. Suddenly I understood that she had loved me very much and that the screaming was her way of trying to make me into the person she felt I should be.

Mother's methods were wrong, but her motives were right. When I understood those facts, I was finally able to release the pain and forgive her. Now when I think of her, it is with fondness. The old sadness and regrets are gone.

Whether your pain comes from your mother, your children, your own self, or someone else, you, too, can be healed. Through information, a willing heart, an open mind, and a clear decision to let go of the past, you can experience forgiveness.

There is a simple progression from hurt to forgiveness.

The first stage is *pain*. Whenever your child rebels or simply disobeys, you are likely to feel the pain of worry or fear. If your child or someone you love lashes out at you, that pain is likely to sharpen to pointed anger or even rage.

Next you must set your mind and *will to forgive*. You must be willing to give up the deceptive power and protection of your anger. Temporarily that will increase your pain, but don't worry. You will overcome it.

The third step is to gain and examine all the *information*. If you are to do a complete job of forgiving, you need to know three things: a) what you may have done to cause hurt, perhaps without even knowing it, b) what prompted someone to hurt you—maybe he or she reacted out of their own pain, and c) a clear perspective on the whole picture.

After information comes *understanding*. When you have all the important information, put it together. Once you understand the "hows" and "whys" of the problem situation, it is much easier to take the next step.

And that next step is to *release it*. A discussion took place in a class Grace took, about just how one could let go of a painful experience, whether it was recent or remote. The leader chose a member who was struggling with the basic issue of forgiveness. Looking directly at him, he demanded, "Bob, take out your handkerchief." Obediently Bob reached for a large, white handkerchief and held it out. "Now," asked the leader, "just drop it!" As the large white cloth fluttered to the floor, the silence became deafening. All clearly knew that the very bottom line was a simple act of the will. "I choose to drop this!"

When you have dropped your fear, anxiety, anger, and stubbornness, you will know the release from pain. You, too, can forgive—yourself and others. The healing will set you free to love and be loved as never before!

And isn't love what life is all about—love and relationships? We hope this book has given you firm ground to stand on and some new handholds for when you feel frustrated. Now it's time for you to take some steps to change your life for the better. We know you can do it. We believe in you!

And the rewards? They will be tremendous—in all areas of your life. Just wait and see.

Appendix

This Mothers' Questionnaire was completed by nearly two hundred women from coast to coast. Perhaps you would like to take it, too. To compare your results with the collated national sampling, see Survey Results.

MOTHERS' QUESTIONNAIRE

I am writing a book which will give mothers a better understanding of themselves and their children, as well as help mothers to change certain negative behavior patterns.

In order to complete the research, I need your assistance. Please answer the following questions. Your anonymous responses are greatly appreciated. Thank you for your time.

Pat Holt

---

1. The ages of my children are:_____

2. Screaming at my children is a problem for me
   ☐ Almost Always   ☐ Sometimes   ☐ Occasionally   ☐ Never

3. I am most likely to scream when (please give an appropriate example):

   _____
   _____
   _____

4. I am least likely to scream when:

   _____

5. I scream at my children when (please number in order of relevance):
   _____ I am pre-menstrual
   _____ I am frustrated with them
   _____ They just won't listen
   _____ I am tired
   _____ They are irresponsible
   _____ I am under a lot of pressure
   _____ They talk back
   _____ I've told them 1000 times
   _____ Too much is happening at once
   _____ I'm angry

6. How do you feel after you scream? (Please give an example)

   _____
   _____
   _____
   _____

7. I scream at my children because (Please number in order of relevance):

_____ It's the only reaction I know

_____ I hope that volume will drive my message home

_____ It makes me feel better

_____ Maybe they will understand how much their behavior effects me

_____ It's better than hitting them

_____ Nobody ever taught me how to deal with misbehavior

_____ It gets results

_____ It gets their attention

8. How do your children react to your screaming? (Please give an example)

_____

_____

_____

_____

9. What do you think is an alternative to screaming? (Please explain your answer)

_____

_____

_____

_____

------------- OPTIONAL INFORMATION -----------

10. Age group:
☐ Under 30   ☐ 30 to 39   ☐ Over 39

11. Highest grade level completed:
☐ High School   ☐ College Credit   ☐ College Degree   ☐ Graduate Credit   ☐ Graduate Degree

12. Currently employed?
☐ No   ☐ Yes (# of hours per week:_____)

13. Average yearly combined family income:
☐ Under $35,000   ☐ $35,000 to $75,000   ☐ Over $75,000

Although responses are anonymous, if you are available for further comment, please include your name, address, telephone number, and best time to call.

Name _____

Street Address _____

City _____ Zip Code _____

Time _____

☎ (_____) _____

On behalf of mothers and children everywhere, thank you.

Survey Results

1. 16% of those surveyed had only one child. 34% had two children, and another 34% had three children. 16% of the mothers had 4 or more children.

   17% had children who were two years old and younger. 24% had children who were between three and five years old. 25% had children in the six-to-nine-year-old bracket. 15% had children who were in the pre-teen, ten-to-twelve age bracket. 19% had children who were thirteen and up.

2. 45% of those surveyed said screaming was *sometimes* a problem for them. 6% said they *almost always* screamed at their kids. 43% said they *occasionally* had problems with screaming, and 6% said they *never* screamed.

3. The top three answers were: a) when stress becomes too great; b) when there are too many demands on my limited time; and c) when I don't feel well.

4. The top four answers were: a) when I am rested; b) when things are calm; c) when the children cooperate without complaining; and d) when I feel I am getting things done.

5. Mothers feel like screaming at their children when (numbered in order from the most frustrating experience to the least frustrating):

   _8_ I am pre-menstrual.

   _6_ I am frustrated with them.

   _5_ They just won't listen.

   _3_ I am tired.

   _9_ They are irresponsible.

   _1_ I am under a lot of pressure.

   _10_ They talk back.

   _4_ I've told them 1,000 times.

   _2_ Too much is happening at once.

   _7_ I'm angry.

6. The top four answers were: a) guilty; b) ashamed or embarrassed; c) better (I released the tension); and d) a sense of power.

7. Mothers scream at their children because (numbered in order from the most common reason to the least common reason):

   __7__ It's the only reaction I know.

   __2__ I hope the volume will drive my message home.

   __5__ It makes me feel better.

   __4__ Maybe they will understand how much their behavior affects me.

   __6__ It's better than hitting them.

   __8__ Nobody ever taught me how to deal with misbehavior.

   __3__ It gets results.

   __1__ It gets their attention.

8. The top four ways children react to screaming are: a) sadness and hurt feelings; b) angry back-talk; c) fear and withdrawal; and d) humiliation and shame.

9. 72% of those surveyed felt the best alternative to screaming was to calm down first, then talk to your kids. 23% felt you should give firm and loving discipline. 5% felt that spanking was the alternative.

10. Only 6% of the mothers surveyed were under thirty. 65% of the mothers were in the thirty to thirty-nine age group. 195 were over thirty-nine. The rest did not reveal their ages.

11. 42% of those surveyed had some college credit, and 33% had completed their college degree. 17% had gone on and done some graduate work. 8% of the mothers had high school diplomas only.

12. 40% of the mothers surveyed were not employed outside the home. Of the 60% who were employed, 15% worked ten hours a week outside the home, 15% worked fifteen hours/week, 28% worked twenty hours/week, and 42% worked full-time (forty hours/week).

Note: It is significant that the women in our study were not aware of how much they screamed until they filled out our Mothers' Questionnaire. A large percentage have told us that just being conscious of their screaming has already helped them to control themselves better. We hope that this encouraging by-product of reading this book will be a large step toward control for you.